A WORD OF THANKS

Thank you for purchasing this book and supporting the work of independent creators. Your encouragement fuels the creativity and passion behind every project we undertake at NineTwo Creations.

As a token of our appreciation, we'd like to invite you to explore our merchandise at www.ninetwocreations.com. Whether you're looking for something unique for yourself or a gift for someone special, we're excited to offer **free shipping** on your order. Simply use the promo code **BOOK** at checkout.

Your support means the world to us, and we're thrilled to have you as part of our growing community. Thank you for being a part of this journey. Here's to the stories we tell, the ideas we share, and the futures we build together!

— NineTwo Creations

GETTING STARTED IN PODCASTING
LAUNCH, GROW, AND MONETIZE YOUR SHOW
BY
Jordan Vance

© Copyright 2024 by NineTwo Creations L.L.C. - All rights reserved.

It is not legal to reproduce, duplicate, or transmit any part of this document in either electronic means or printed format. Recording of this publication is strictly prohibited.

First Edition

Published by NineTwo Creations L.L.C.

For permission requests, contact the publisher at ninetwocreations@gmail.com

This book is intended for informational purposes only. The author and publisher make no representations or warranties regarding the accuracy, applicability, or completeness of the contents. The reader is advised to consult with a professional where appropriate.

TABLE OF CONTENTS

Introduction 1

    Chapter 1: The Power of Podcasting 3

    Chapter 2: Finding Your Niche 6

    Chapter 3: Naming and Branding Your Podcast 12

    Chapter 4: Choosing a Format and Episode Structure 17

    Chapter 5: Essential Equipment and Setup 23

    Chapter 6: Recording and Editing Your First Episode 29

    Chapter 7: Hosting and Distributing Your Podcast 36

    Chapter 8: Monetizing Your Podcast 43

    Chapter 9: Marketing and Growing Your Audience 50

    Chapter 10: Sustaining Your Podcast Journey 59

A Word from the Author 66

Introduction

Hi, I'm Jordan Vance. For years, I immersed myself in the world of live streaming—observing, learning, and uncovering what separates the successful streamers from those still searching for their audience. That journey was an incredible experience, filled with insights about building communities, connecting with viewers, and mastering the art of digital storytelling. It ultimately led to the creation of *Getting Started in Streaming*, a guide designed to help aspiring streamers carve their path and thrive in a competitive industry.

But as I explored the ever-changing landscape of content creation, my curiosity began to shift toward another exciting medium: podcasting. Podcasting, like streaming, is a platform for connection. Where streaming thrives in its immediacy and interactivity, podcasting offers something equally powerful—a chance to slow down, dive deep, and create timeless content that resonates long after it's released.

Making the transition from streaming to podcasting felt natural to me. The lessons I learned about engaging an audience, maintaining authenticity, and staying consistent applied seamlessly. But podcasting also brought its own set of unique challenges and opportunities, ones I've embraced with the same curiosity and passion that fueled my streaming journey.

Now, with *Getting Started in Podcasting: Your Guide to Sharing Your Voice and Building an Audience*, I'm here to do for podcasting what I did for streaming: provide a comprehensive roadmap to help creators find their voice, connect with listeners, and grow something meaningful. This book is designed to guide you through the essentials of podcasting, whether you're transitioning from another platform, like streaming, or diving into this medium for the first time.

We'll cover it all—choosing your niche, building your brand, recording your first episode, and engaging with your audience. Along the way, I'll share practical advice, real-world examples, and actionable strategies to help you create a podcast that feels authentic and impactful.

Podcasting is an exciting journey, filled with opportunities to connect, create, and leave a lasting legacy. It demands preparation, consistency, and heart—but the rewards are more than worth it. By the time you finish this book, you'll feel confident in your ability to share your voice, connect with your audience, and build a podcast that truly matters.

Let's get started. Your voice deserves to be heard, and the world is waiting to listen.

Chapter 1: The Power of Podcasting

Podcasting has become one of the most dynamic and accessible mediums for sharing ideas, stories, and expertise with the world. What began as a niche corner of the internet has grown into a global phenomenon. Today, there are over 2.5 million podcasts, and more than 460 million people tune in regularly. With such an expansive reach, podcasting has the potential to connect creators and listeners across borders, time zones, and interests like never before.

One of the most appealing aspects of podcasting is its accessibility. Unlike traditional media, which often requires expensive equipment or a team of professionals, podcasting levels the playing field. With a basic microphone, some editing software, and a good idea, anyone can create a show. It doesn't matter if you're recording in a high-tech studio or a corner of your living room—if you have something to say, podcasting gives you a platform.

The stories of successful podcasters highlight the transformative power of this medium. Joe Rogan, for instance, started his podcast as a casual side project, and it eventually became one of the most downloaded shows in history, earning him a multi-million-dollar licensing deal with Spotify. Similarly, Crime Junkie began as two friends sharing true crime stories and grew into a chart-topping sensation with a devoted following. These successes show that podcasting isn't just for celebrities or tech-savvy entrepreneurs—it's a medium for anyone willing to invest their creativity and effort.

Podcasting's rise reflects a fundamental shift in how people consume content. Audiences crave authentic voices and niche interests—things traditional media often overlooks. With podcasting, you're not competing for the broadest audience; instead, you're finding the right audience, one that aligns with your unique message. That's what makes it so powerful: no matter how specific your interest, there's a space for you to create and connect.

Podcasting offers a wealth of benefits for individuals and businesses alike, making it one of the most versatile and rewarding mediums in today's digital landscape. Whether you're a seasoned entrepreneur, an industry expert, or someone with a passion to share, podcasting provides opportunities to connect, grow, and even generate income.

For individuals, podcasting can be a platform to build authority in a specific field. Sharing your expertise through engaging episodes not only educates your audience but also positions you as a thought leader. Over time, this credibility can open doors to speaking engagements, collaborations, or consulting opportunities. For instance, consider the impact of podcasts like

How I Built This by Guy Raz, which highlights entrepreneurial stories while cementing its host's reputation as a master interviewer in the business space.

Podcasting also excels at fostering a sense of community. Unlike other forms of content, podcasts create an intimate connection between the host and the listener. Your voice becomes a trusted presence in their lives—whether they're commuting, cooking, or unwinding. This connection encourages loyalty and engagement, which can translate into a dedicated fan base. Many podcasters build thriving online communities around their shows, connecting listeners through social media groups, live events, or listener Q&A episodes.

For businesses, podcasts are a strategic tool to reach customers in a genuine, value-driven way. Instead of interrupting a listener's experience with traditional ads, businesses can produce content that informs and entertains while subtly reinforcing their brand message. A podcast on sustainable living, for example, could naturally align with a brand offering eco-friendly products, fostering trust and interest without a hard sell.

The potential for passive income is another compelling benefit of podcasting. While it takes time and effort to build a loyal audience, monetization opportunities are abundant. Sponsorships allow companies to pay for ad slots during episodes, typically based on the number of downloads. For creators, platforms like Patreon offer a way to secure direct listener support through donations or paid subscriptions. Additionally, podcasters can create and sell merchandise, host paid live shows, or offer premium content to further diversify revenue streams.

Podcasting's benefits aren't limited to financial rewards. It's also a powerful medium for personal growth. The process of creating episodes—researching topics, refining communication skills, and engaging with feedback—fosters creativity and confidence. Podcasters often report feeling more connected to their passions and communities, making the endeavor as fulfilling as it is impactful.

Whether your goal is to build a brand, expand your reach, or simply share your voice, podcasting offers unparalleled opportunities to grow and thrive in ways that are authentic and meaningful.

Podcasting is more than just a medium for entertainment or education—it's a revolution in how stories are told, ideas are shared, and voices are heard. What makes podcasting truly remarkable is its ability to democratize content creation. Unlike traditional forms of media, which often require substantial investments and depend on gatekeepers to decide what gets published, podcasting strips away these barriers. With just a microphone, an idea, and a willingness to learn, anyone can join the conversation.

This openness has led to an explosion of diversity in content. Podcasts now exist on virtually every topic imaginable, from astrophysics to gardening, from personal development to niche cultural phenomena. Creators no longer need to cater to the broadest audience; instead, they can focus on their passions and connect with listeners who share their enthusiasm. This authenticity not only strengthens the bond between hosts and audiences but also encourages creativity and experimentation.

At its core, podcasting is an invitation. It invites creators to take the leap and share their unique perspectives. It invites listeners to explore new worlds and discover voices they wouldn't have encountered otherwise. The ripple effects of this democratization are profound: more ideas are being exchanged, more stories are being told, and more communities are being built.

So, whether you're dreaming of inspiring others, growing your business, or simply sharing your passions with the world, podcasting offers a chance to make your mark. It's a platform where your voice matters—where every creator has the potential to reach, impact, and inspire. All you need to do is press "record" and step into the world of possibilities waiting for you.

Chapter 2: Finding Your Niche

Starting a podcast is a thrilling venture, full of possibility and creative freedom. But before you jump in, there's one essential question you need to answer: Why are you doing this? Your "why" is the foundation of your podcasting journey. It's what will guide your decisions, shape your content, and sustain your motivation during challenging moments. Without it, you risk losing direction—or worse, burning out before you truly get started.

For some, the "why" is clear from the start. Perhaps you're a small business owner hoping to attract new clients or an expert in your field looking to share your knowledge with a wider audience. Maybe you want to raise awareness for a cause close to your heart or simply share your passion for a niche hobby. For others, the motivation might not be so obvious right away. That's okay too. What matters is taking the time to think it through. Podcasting isn't just about speaking into a microphone—it's about purposefully connecting with others through the...

Knowing your "why" also helps set the tone for your podcast. If your goal is personal fulfillment, the pressure to achieve external success fades into the background. If you're podcasting to generate income or build authority, you can focus on strategies to attract sponsors or engage a professional audience. Clarity on your purpose will allow you to create content that feels authentic while staying aligned with your long-term goals.

Defining your "why" isn't just about motivation; it's a practical exercise. Let's say you're a graphic designer considering a podcast to share insights about your industry. If your "why" is to connect with fellow designers, you might focus on discussing design trends, tools, and techniques. If your "why" is to attract clients, you'd tailor your content to appeal to business owners or entrepreneurs who need design services. The clearer your purpose, the more focused your content will be—and the easier it will be to reach the right audience.

Many podcasters find their purpose by asking a few simple but powerful questions:

- What topics light you up and make you want to keep talking, even when no one's listening?
- What unique experiences, skills, or perspectives can you bring to the table?
- Who do you want to connect with, and what value can you offer them?
- What do you hope to achieve with your podcast, both personally and professionally?

For example, someone with a passion for sustainability might start a podcast to teach listeners how to reduce their environmental footprint. Their "why" could be as broad as promoting eco-friendly living or as specific as inspiring change in their local community. Understanding this motivation would help them choose the right tone, format, and topics for their episodes.

The "why" also keeps you grounded when challenges arise. Podcasting can be time-consuming and sometimes discouraging, especially when growth feels slow. A strong sense of purpose reminds you why you started and pushes you to keep going. Many podcasters experience what's known as "podfade," where enthusiasm wanes, and episodes become less frequent until they stop altogether. Knowing your "why" acts as a buffer against this, giving you the resilience to weather setbacks and stay consistent.

Clarity of purpose also helps you manage expectations. It's easy to get caught up in the glamour of podcasting success stories—those tales of creators who earn millions or rack up millions of downloads overnight. But for most podcasters, success looks different. It might mean reaching a dedicated group of listeners who resonate deeply with your message. It could mean landing an exciting business opportunity, growing your personal network, or simply knowing that your voice made an impact on someone's life.

One real-life example is *Side Hustle School* by Chris Guillebeau. The "why" behind this podcast is clear: to inspire and empower people to create additional income streams without quitting their day jobs. By focusing on practical, actionable advice and relatable success stories, Guillebeau has built a loyal audience of aspiring entrepreneurs. His clarity of purpose has not only kept the content consistent but also positioned the podcast as a valuable resource for listeners with a shared goal.

Another example is the podcast *Ten Percent Happier* by Dan Harris, which explores mindfulness and meditation in a relatable way. Harris's "why" stems from his personal journey to manage stress and anxiety, and his episodes are shaped by his desire to help others navigate similar challenges. This clear purpose is evident in the show's tone, guests, and topics, which focus on accessible tools for improving mental health.

Finding your "why" is the first step in carving out your niche, and it's also a deeply personal process. It doesn't have to be grand or earth-shattering—it just has to matter to you. Whether it's to entertain, educate, advocate, or connect, your purpose is what makes your podcast uniquely yours. It's the spark that will sustain you through the long hours of planning, recording, editing, and promoting.

Before moving on to brainstorming ideas or picking a format, take the time to write down your "why." Reflect on it, refine it, and make it your north star. The clearer your purpose, the easier it will be to build a podcast that resonates—not just with your audience but with yourself. Podcasting isn't about perfection; it's about intention. And the best intentions always start with understanding why.

Once you've defined your "why," the next step is choosing a niche for your podcast. This is where your vision starts to take shape. Your niche is the intersection of what excites you and what your audience finds valuable. It's the sweet spot where your passion meets purpose. A clearly defined niche not only helps you create focused, engaging content but also makes it easier for the right listeners to find your show.

In podcasting, specificity is your greatest ally. While it might seem counterintuitive, trying to appeal to everyone usually leads to appealing to no one. Instead, focus on a specific topic or audience. For instance, instead of creating a general podcast about fitness, you could narrow it down to fitness tips for busy parents or training strategies for marathon runners. The more specific you are, the easier it is to stand out in a crowded space.

Successful niche podcasts prove this point time and again. Take *Sleep With Me*, a podcast designed to help listeners fall asleep. Host Drew Ackerman tells meandering, low-energy bedtime stories that are deliberately boring. It's a highly specific concept, but it resonates deeply with people who struggle with insomnia. Similarly, *The Pen Addict* caters to a surprisingly passionate community of pen and stationery enthusiasts. These shows thrive not because they appeal to a massive audience, but because t...

Once you've identified your niche, it's time to brainstorm episode ideas. Start by making a list of questions, challenges, or topics that your target audience might care about. If your podcast is about sustainable living, for example, potential episodes could include:

- "10 Easy Ways to Reduce Plastic Waste"
- "How to Start Composting in an Apartment"
- "Interview with an Expert: The Future of Renewable Energy"

If you're struggling for ideas, try these brainstorming exercises:

- **Explore Your Expertise**: Think about what you know well or what you're passionate about. What lessons or insights could you share?
- **Survey the Competition**: Listen to podcasts in your chosen genre and identify gaps. Are there topics they're not covering or perspectives they're missing?
- **Ask Your Audience**: If you already have a small following (on social media or elsewhere), ask them what they'd like to learn or hear about.

Your goal during this phase isn't to perfect every idea—it's to generate a large list of possibilities. Once you have a list, group similar topics together and look for recurring themes.

This will help you develop a structure for your episodes and identify potential series or recurring segments.

Before committing fully to your niche, it's worth testing your ideas. This doesn't mean you need to launch your podcast right away. Instead, start small with these strategies:

- **Record Demo Episodes**: Pick one or two topics from your brainstorming list and record short, informal episodes. Don't worry about perfection—focus on the content and flow. This exercise will help you determine whether you enjoy discussing the topic and if it feels sustainable.
- **Seek Feedback**: Share your demo episodes with a trusted group of friends, colleagues, or potential listeners. Ask for honest feedback: Did they find the content interesting? Was it clear and engaging? Would they listen to more?
- **Pilot on Social Media**: Use your social media channels to test ideas. Share a short video or post about a potential episode topic and gauge the response. If a particular post generates lots of engagement or questions, it's a good sign that the topic has traction.

Testing your ideas is a low-pressure way to refine your vision and make adjustments before committing to a full-fledged launch.

Looking at real-world examples can spark inspiration and show how specificity can lead to success. Here are a few standout niche podcasts:

- **Side Hustle School**: This podcast focuses exclusively on actionable ideas for starting side hustles. By zeroing in on a specific goal—helping listeners create extra income streams—it has attracted a loyal audience of aspiring entrepreneurs.
- **Wine for Normal People**: Instead of catering to wine connoisseurs, this podcast demystifies the world of wine for everyday people. Its approachable tone and relatable content make it stand out in a niche that can sometimes feel intimidating.
- **Lore**: Host Aaron Mahnke shares eerie historical tales in a unique, storytelling format. By focusing on folklore and its historical context, Mahnke carved out a niche that appeals to history buffs and horror fans alike.

Each of these podcasts started with a clear, specific idea and stayed true to its niche. Their success demonstrates the power of aligning your passion with your audience's interests.

As you brainstorm and test, you might find yourself drawn to more than one niche. That's normal! However, it's important to refine your focus before launching. Trying to cover too many topics can confuse your audience and dilute your message.

One way to refine your niche is by considering your ideal listener. Who are they? What are their challenges, goals, or interests? The more clearly you can picture your audience, the easier it will be to create content that speaks directly to them.

For example, let's say you're passionate about fitness, nutrition, and mental health. Instead of creating a broad wellness podcast, you might narrow it down to "mental health strategies for athletes" or "nutrition hacks for busy professionals." A focused niche doesn't limit your creativity—it provides a framework that ensures your content stays relevant and engaging.

Choosing a niche isn't just about the launch—it's about sustainability. Podcasting is a long-term commitment, and your niche should be something you're excited to explore over time. Ask yourself: Can you see yourself talking about this topic in a year? Five years? If the answer is yes, you're on the right track.

Finding your niche is an iterative process. It's okay if your ideas evolve or shift as you move forward. What matters is starting with a clear focus and a willingness to adapt. Podcasting rewards those who combine passion with persistence, and finding your niche is the first step toward building something truly impactful.

When it comes to podcasting, your biggest strength isn't expensive equipment, celebrity guests, or even polished production. It's *you*. Your unique perspective, experiences, and passions are what will set your podcast apart from the thousands of others out there. No one else has your exact story, your voice, or your combination of interests. That's your differentiator, and it's what your audience will connect with most deeply.

Passion fuels sustainability. Podcasting is a long-term endeavor, and while trends come and go, your enthusiasm for your topic will keep you showing up week after week. This is why choosing a niche that genuinely excites you is so critical. If you're talking about something you love, the work feels less like a grind and more like a creative outlet. Your passion will be evident in every episode, and that energy is contagious—listeners will notice, and they'll keep coming back for more.

Uniqueness drives connection. In podcasting, authenticity isn't just a buzzword; it's a necessity. Listeners don't just want content; they want connection. They're tuning in because they feel a sense of camaraderie with you as a host. When you lean into what makes you different—whether it's your quirky sense of humor, your unconventional career path, or your deeply personal perspective—you give listeners a reason to choose your podcast over others.

Consider the podcast *My Favorite Murder*. On paper, it's a true crime show, and there are plenty of those. But what makes it stand out is the hosts' unique approach. Karen Kilgariff and Georgia Hardstark blend humor, empathy, and personal anecdotes into their storytelling.

They're unapologetically themselves, and that authenticity has earned them a fiercely loyal fanbase.

Similarly, *The Happiness Lab* with Dr. Laurie Santos takes the concept of exploring happiness—a topic covered extensively in books, blogs, and videos—and filters it through her academic background in psychology. Her unique perspective and deep knowledge make the show both engaging and credible.

Your podcast doesn't need to reinvent the wheel; it just needs to reflect *you*. Even if your niche is a well-trodden one, your perspective can bring something fresh to the table. Maybe you have a personal story that adds depth to your topic, or perhaps you approach it with a tone or style that feels different from others in the space.

As you focus on your unique perspective, remember that podcasting isn't about perfection. It's about authenticity. You don't need to sound like a professional broadcaster or have every detail ironed out before you start. Listeners are drawn to real, relatable hosts—not flawless performances. Embrace your quirks, lean into your strengths, and don't be afraid to share your story.

Finding your voice as a podcaster is a journey, and it evolves over time. What matters most is starting from a place of passion and authenticity. Be willing to experiment, adapt, and grow. Your audience will grow with you, and the connections you build will become one of the most rewarding aspects of your podcasting journey.

As you wrap up your planning and prepare to hit record, take a moment to reflect on what makes your podcast truly *yours*. What excites you about your topic? What unique perspective are you bringing? What do you hope to share with your audience? These answers will guide you, sustain you, and set you apart in the world of podcasting.

The beauty of podcasting is that there's no one-size-fits-all formula. It's a space where creativity thrives, where niche topics find passionate audiences, and where every voice has the potential to be heard. By focusing on your passions and sharing your unique perspective, you're not just creating a podcast—you're building something meaningful, something that reflects who you are and what you care about.

Your audience is waiting. All you have to do is show up as yourself and start the conversation.

Chapter 3: Naming and Branding Your Podcast

Choosing the right name and building a strong brand are two of the most important steps you'll take as a podcaster. They're the first things potential listeners encounter, the elements that make them pause, click, and decide whether your show is worth their time. A memorable name and compelling branding don't just attract attention—they set the tone for your podcast and create the foundation for how your audience connects with it.

Think of your podcast's name as its handshake. It's the first impression you make, and just like a good handshake, it should feel confident, clear, and genuine. A great podcast name tells listeners what your show is about while sparking curiosity. It's specific enough to stand out but broad enough to give you room to grow. The best names stick in people's minds, making it easy for them to recommend your show to a friend or search for it later.

Branding takes this a step further. It's not just about how your podcast looks or sounds—it's the story you're telling and the emotional connection you're building with your audience. Your branding encompasses everything from your artwork and music to the tone of your voice and the way you engage with listeners. It's the unspoken promise you make about what they can expect from your show.

Consider some of the most successful podcasts. *The Daily* is succinct and authoritative, perfectly fitting its role as a daily news briefing from *The New York Times*. On the other hand, *Armchair Expert* by Dax Shepard is casual, inviting, and a little self-deprecating, which reflects the show's candid, conversational approach. Each name and brand is tailored to its audience, immediately communicating the essence of the podcast.

Getting your name and branding right isn't just about aesthetics—it's about creating a sense of trust and recognition. In a sea of podcasts competing for attention, your name and brand are the tools that make listeners stop scrolling and press play. They're your way of saying, "This is who I am, this is what I'm about, and this is why you should join me."

A memorable name and strong branding don't guarantee success, but they do open the door. They make the first connection, inviting people into your world. And once they're there, your content can do the rest. Before you record your first episode, take the time to think deeply about what you want your podcast to represent. Your name and branding are more than just details—they're the foundation of your podcast's identity.

Choosing the right name for your podcast and building its brand can feel daunting, but it's also one of the most exciting steps in the process. This is where your vision starts to take shape, transforming from an idea into something tangible. Your name and branding will act as the first point of contact for potential listeners, so it's worth investing the time to get it right. Here's how you can approach it strategically while keeping your creativity alive.

Begin by letting your imagination run wild. Sit down with a notebook or open a blank document, and start jotting down every idea that comes to mind. Don't filter yourself or worry about perfection—this is your creative playground. The goal is to generate as many ideas as possible, trusting that some will rise to the surface as winners. Your initial brainstorming session is about exploring possibilities and capturing the essence of your podcast in words.

Start by thinking deeply about what your podcast is all about. Consider its themes, topics, or tone. Is it an educational show designed to teach and inspire? A lighthearted series aimed at entertaining? Or perhaps a niche exploration of a subject you're deeply passionate about? Use keywords that resonate with your topic and vibe. For example, if you're planning a podcast on financial independence, words like "freedom," "wealth," or "hustle" might capture your focus. These words can later evolve into a na...

Next, think about your audience. Who are you speaking to, and what do they value? If your audience consists of parents, you might include terms like "family," "mom," or "dad." For entrepreneurs, words like "startup," "scale," or "success" might feel relevant. By keeping your audience in mind, you ensure your name resonates with the people you want to reach.

Wordplay can be a game-changer. Clever puns, alliteration, or unexpected combinations of words often make a name more memorable. Take inspiration from names like *Crime Junkie*, which combines intrigue with a playful twist, or *Stuff You Should Know*, which is both inviting and informative. Play around with language, experimenting with how words sound and fit together. Sometimes, a little creativity is all it takes to make your name stand out in a crowded directory.

Simplicity is key. In a world where attention spans are short, shorter names tend to stick better. A name that's easy to remember and quick to search gives you an advantage. Aim for two to five words—enough to convey your idea without becoming unwieldy. Avoid overly complicated phrases or jargon that might confuse your audience.

Once you've brainstormed a list of potential podcast names, the next step is to refine your options and choose one that truly represents your show. Narrow it down to a few favorites that feel aligned with your podcast's purpose and tone. Then, test them out by sharing with friends, family, or even a small group of your target audience. Hearing their reactions can provide valuable insights—sometimes, what sounds great in your head might come across differently to others. Pay attention to which names spark interest and curiosity, as well as any that might be confusing or fail to convey your podcast's essence.

After gathering feedback, it's time to check the availability of your top choices. This is a critical step—you don't want to fall in love with a name only to discover that it's already taken or too similar to an existing podcast. Start by searching major podcast directories like Apple Podcasts, Spotify, and Google Podcasts. Type in your potential names to see if any similar shows already exist. If they do, consider how this might impact your audience's ability to find your show or whether it could cau...

Beyond podcast directories, think about how your name will function across other platforms. Is the domain name available for a website? Can you secure matching handles on social media? Tools like Namecheap or GoDaddy can help you search for domain availability, while a quick check on platforms like Twitter, Instagram, and Facebook will tell you if the name is free for use. Consistency across platforms strengthens your brand and makes it easier for listeners to connect with you.

It's also worth considering potential trademark issues. If your chosen name is too similar to an existing podcast or brand, you might run into legal trouble later. A quick search using the United States Patent and Trademark Office (USPTO) database—or your country's equivalent—can help you avoid potential headaches. Even if you're not planning to trademark your name immediately, ensuring it's unique and legally safe from the start is a smart move.

Once you've landed on the perfect name, the next step is to bring your brand to life through visuals. Your podcast artwork is often the first thing potential listeners will see, and it needs to grab their attention while clearly communicating what your show is about.

Keep your design simple and impactful. Podcast artwork is often displayed as a small thumbnail, so avoid cluttered layouts or text that's difficult to read at smaller sizes. Instead, focus on bold, clear imagery that reflects the essence of your podcast. If your show is a comedy, opt for bright, playful colors and fun visuals. For a true crime podcast, darker tones and dramatic elements might be more fitting. The key is to match your artwork to your podcast's theme and tone.

High-quality images are essential. Most podcast platforms, including Apple Podcasts, have specific requirements for artwork, such as a resolution of 3000 x 3000 pixels. Ensuring your artwork meets these standards not only avoids rejection but also ensures it looks sharp and professional on all devices.

If you're comfortable with design tools, platforms like Canva provide easy-to-use templates specifically for podcast artwork. On the other hand, if design isn't your strong suit or you want a more polished look, consider hiring a freelance designer. Websites like Fiverr and 99Designs offer access to professionals who can bring your vision to life. Whatever route you choose, make sure the final design resonates with the identity you're building for your podcast.

Branding doesn't stop with your artwork—it extends to every element of your podcast, from your color palette and fonts to the music that introduces each episode. Colors evoke emotions and set the tone for your brand. A motivational podcast might use vibrant, energetic shades like orange or yellow to convey positivity and drive. Meanwhile, a mindfulness podcast could opt for calming blues and greens to reflect its serene vibe. Choose two or three core colors and use them consistently across your artwork,...

Fonts also play a crucial role in shaping your podcast's identity. A bold, modern font might suit a tech-focused show, while a handwritten or script font could work beautifully for a storytelling podcast. Whatever style you choose, ensure it's legible and pairs well with your other branding elements. Fonts should enhance your message, not distract from it.

Finally, consider the role of music in creating your podcast's atmosphere. Your intro and outro music act as the soundtrack to your show, setting the stage for your content and leaving a lasting impression on your audience. Upbeat tracks work well for high-energy podcasts, while softer, ambient music might suit a reflective or meditative show. Resources like AudioJungle and Epidemic Sound offer a wide range of royalty-free music, making it easy to find the perfect track to match your podcast's vibe.

Bringing all these elements together—your name, artwork, colors, fonts, and music—creates a cohesive brand that not only attracts listeners but also builds trust and recognition. Think of your branding as the story you're telling before anyone presses play. Every detail contributes to that story, helping potential listeners decide whether your podcast is the right fit for them.

Remember, branding is an ongoing process. You might find yourself tweaking your artwork, experimenting with new music, or refining your tone as your podcast evolves. That's okay. The most important thing is to start with a strong foundation that reflects who you are and what your podcast stands for. When your branding feels authentic and aligned with your vision, it will resonate with your audience—and that's what truly matters.

A tagline is an optional but effective way to reinforce your podcast's message. It's a short phrase or sentence that sums up what your show is about. For instance, *Side Hustle School* uses "Learn how to start a side hustle without quitting your day job." A strong tagline can clarify your purpose and entice new listeners.

When you've finalized your name, artwork, and branding elements, take a step back and assess everything as a whole. Does it feel cohesive? Does it reflect your podcast's identity? Most importantly, does it excite you? Your branding should not only attract listeners but also make you proud of the creative work you're putting into the world.

Remember, branding is an evolving process. You don't have to get it perfect on day one. Many podcasters tweak their artwork, music, or taglines over time as their shows grow and develop. What matters most is starting with a strong foundation that captures the essence of your podcast and sets you up for success.

By investing in thoughtful naming and branding, you're not just creating a podcast—you're building an experience that will resonate with your audience long after they press play.

Chapter 4: Choosing a Format and Episode Structure

The beauty of podcasting lies in its flexibility. There are no hard-and-fast rules for how a podcast should look or sound. Instead, the format you choose should reflect your goals, align with your personality, and cater to your audience. Choosing the right format sets the stage for your show's identity and makes it easier to plan episodes that flow naturally.

Podcast formats generally fall into a few broad categories. The most common is the interview format, where the host invites guests to share their expertise or stories. This style works well if you enjoy connecting with others and want to bring diverse perspectives to your audience. Shows like *The Tim Ferriss Show* and *How I Built This* have popularized this approach, demonstrating how interviews can dive deep into fascinating topics while keeping listeners engaged.

Another popular choice is the solo podcast, where you take center stage as the host and storyteller. This format works well for sharing expertise, telling personal stories, or delivering insights in a straightforward way. If you're confident in your voice and have a knack for keeping the energy up, this format allows you to connect directly with your audience. Podcasts like *The Happiness Lab* with Dr. Laurie Santos or *Side Hustle School* are excellent examples of solo shows that educate and inspire.

For those who enjoy collaboration, the co-hosted format can be a fantastic choice. Co-hosts bring a conversational dynamic that feels natural and engaging, allowing for humor, banter, or debate. Shows like *Crime Junkie* or *My Favorite Murder* thrive on the chemistry between their hosts, creating a sense of intimacy that draws listeners in. Co-hosting also splits the workload, which can make the production process more manageable. However, it's important to choose a co-host who shares your vision and ...

Beyond these main formats, there are also more specialized options. Narrative storytelling podcasts, such as *Serial* or *Lore*, use a highly produced, scripted style to guide listeners through a story. This format often requires more planning and editing but can create an immersive experience for the audience. Similarly, panel discussions bring multiple voices to the table, offering diverse perspectives on a topic. This approach can be particularly effective for podcasts covering news, current e...

Choosing the right format begins with asking yourself a few key questions:

- What kind of energy do you want to bring to your show?
- How much time can you dedicate to planning, recording, and editing?
- Do you prefer working solo, collaborating with others, or a mix of both?

Your answers will guide you toward a format that feels sustainable and authentic. Remember, your choice isn't set in stone. Many podcasters experiment with multiple formats before settling into what works best. The goal is to find a structure that aligns with your strengths and allows your content to shine.

The format you choose is the foundation of your podcast, but it's also a reflection of your unique style. Whether you're interviewing experts, sharing solo insights, or collaborating with a co-host, your format should amplify your voice and connect with your audience.

Once you've chosen a format for your podcast, the next step is crafting episodes that captivate your audience from start to finish. A well-structured episode keeps listeners engaged, makes your content flow smoothly, and ensures your message resonates. While every podcast is unique, there are universal building blocks you can use to create a strong foundation for your episodes.

The first moments of your episode are crucial. This is your chance to grab the listener's attention and convince them to stick around. A good hook can set the tone, build anticipation, and establish what your episode is about. Think of it as your opening pitch—a promise to your audience that the next 20, 30, or 60 minutes will be worth their time.

Start by briefly introducing the episode's topic and why it matters. For example, if your podcast is about productivity, you might say, "Today, we're diving into three proven strategies to reclaim your mornings and start the day with focus and clarity." If you're hosting an interview, tease the guest's expertise: "Our guest today is a bestselling author who's cracked the code on balancing work and life—and they're here to share their secrets."

Adding a personal anecdote or an intriguing fact can also create a compelling hook. For instance, starting with, "Did you know that the average person wastes over two hours a day on distractions?" instantly gives your audience something to latch onto while setting up your topic.

After the hook, transition into your introduction. This is where you establish context and outline what listeners can expect from the episode. Keep it brief but informative. If you have recurring segments or themes, now is the time to mention them. For example:

"Welcome to *The Creative Edge*, the podcast where we explore how to unlock your inner artist and take bold steps toward your creative goals. In today's episode, we'll explore how successful creators stay inspired, featuring insights from our special guest."

Your intro doesn't have to be static. While some podcasters stick to a consistent script, others adjust their intros slightly for each episode to reflect the unique content or tone of the day.

The core content is the heart of your episode. This is where you deliver on the promise you made in your hook and intro. Whether you're sharing a story, interviewing a guest, or breaking down actionable tips, the key is to keep your audience engaged by maintaining a logical flow and avoiding unnecessary tangents.

- **Plan Your Talking Points**: Before recording, outline the main points you want to cover. If you're narrating solo, think of your episode as a journey—what's the starting point, where are you leading your listeners, and what's the destination?

- **Ask Thoughtful Questions**: If you're hosting an interview, craft open-ended questions that encourage your guest to share stories and insights. Avoid simple yes-or-no questions. Instead, ask things like, "What inspired you to pursue this path?" or "Can you walk us through a moment when everything changed for you?"

- **Include Examples and Stories**: People connect with stories more than abstract concepts. Use anecdotes, case studies, or personal experiences to illustrate your points. For instance, if you're explaining productivity hacks, share how they've worked in your life or for someone you know.

- **Engage the Listener**: Make your audience feel involved. Ask rhetorical questions or include moments that encourage reflection: "What's one habit you could change right now to make your mornings more productive?" This creates a sense of dialogue, even in a solo episode.

- **Pace Yourself**: Pay attention to the pacing of your content. If you're sharing a lot of information, break it into smaller segments and use natural pauses or transitions to help your audience absorb it.

Transitions are the glue that holds your episode together. Without them, your content can feel disjointed or abrupt. Smooth transitions help guide your listeners from one point to the next, maintaining flow and keeping them engaged.

- **Use Bridge Phrases**: Phrases like "That brings us to…" or "Another important aspect to consider is…" signal a shift in focus while keeping the narrative moving.

- **Recap Key Points**: If you're moving between segments, briefly summarize what you've covered and set up what's coming next. For example, "Now that we've discussed the basics of goal-setting, let's dive into some advanced techniques to keep you on track."

- **Incorporate Music or Sound Effects**: Many podcasters use short music clips or sound effects to mark transitions. These audio cues help listeners follow the structure of your episode and add a layer of polish to your production.

Just as a strong opening sets the tone, a strong conclusion leaves a lasting impression. Your conclusion is your chance to reinforce your main message and give listeners a clear takeaway.

- **Summarize the Episode**: Recap the key points you've covered to reinforce their importance. For instance, "Today, we talked about three strategies to reclaim your mornings: prioritizing tasks, eliminating distractions, and creating a simple morning ritual."

- **Include a Call to Action**: Encourage your listeners to take the next step. This could be subscribing to your podcast, leaving a review, visiting your website, or trying out a tip you shared. For example, "If you found today's episode helpful, make sure to subscribe so you don't miss our upcoming series on creative goal-setting."

- **End on a Memorable Note**: Close with a compelling quote, an encouraging message, or a teaser for the next episode. For instance, "Remember, every morning is a chance to start fresh. Let's make tomorrow count. See you next week!"

While these elements form the backbone of a well-structured episode, don't be afraid to experiment and adapt to what feels natural for you and your audience. Over time, you'll develop a rhythm and style that make your episodes distinct. Whether your show is a deep dive into technical topics or a casual conversation between friends, structuring your episodes thoughtfully will help you build trust and keep listeners coming back for more.

Podcasting is as unique as the individuals who create it. There's no perfect formula, no universal structure that guarantees success. What works for one podcast may not work for another, and that's part of the beauty of the medium—it's yours to shape, experiment with, and grow into.

As you start creating, remember that it's okay to try different formats and structures. You might begin with a solo podcast, sharing your expertise and stories, and later decide to bring on guests for interviews. Or you may find that a co-host adds the conversational dynamic you didn't realize your show was missing. The key is to remain flexible and open to change.

Think of your podcast as a work in progress. Your first episodes will likely look and feel different from those you create a year from now, and that's a good thing. Podcasting is a learning experience, and each episode is an opportunity to refine your style, adapt to your audience's preferences, and discover what truly works for you.

Consider the stories of successful podcasters. Many started with minimal equipment, a rough idea, and plenty of trial and error. *The Tim Ferriss Show* didn't begin as the polished, high-profile interview podcast it is today—it evolved over time as Tim experimented with formats and learned what resonated with his audience. Similarly, *Side Hustle School* by Chris Guillebeau grew out of a specific goal—to share actionable side hustle ideas—and refined its format through consistent iteration.

Don't be afraid to listen to your audience. Their feedback can be a valuable guide as you navigate your podcasting journey. If listeners love your deep dives into specific topics but tune out during longer interviews, consider adjusting your format to prioritize what keeps them engaged. On the flip side, if you're passionate about a particular structure or approach, don't hesitate to stick with it—even if it's unconventional. Authenticity is more important than conforming to trends.

Above all, trust yourself. Your voice, perspective, and creativity are what make your podcast unique. Whether you're narrating solo, hosting interviews, or crafting intricate storytelling episodes, lean into the style that feels most natural to you. Podcasting is an art form, and like any art, it thrives on experimentation and individuality.

So, as you create your first episodes, let go of the pressure to get everything perfect right away. Focus on what excites you, what aligns with your goals, and what feels authentic. Embrace the journey, and know that each step—whether it's a seamless episode or a lesson learned—brings you closer to finding your rhythm.

There's no one-size-fits-all format for podcasting, and that's precisely why it's such an empowering medium. It allows you to create on your terms, connect with your audience in meaningful ways, and evolve as a creator. Your podcast is your story, your voice, and your vision. The rest is yours to figure out—and that's where the magic happens.

Getting Started in Podcasting

Chapter 5: Essential Equipment and Setup

Starting a podcast doesn't require a high-end studio or thousands of dollars' worth of equipment. In fact, some of the most successful podcasters began with nothing more than a simple microphone and a quiet space to record. That said, having the right tools can elevate the quality of your show and make the recording process smoother. Understanding the basics of podcasting equipment will help you create episodes that sound professional without breaking the bank.

At the heart of your setup is the microphone. This is your primary tool, the piece of equipment that will have the biggest impact on your audio quality. There are two main types of microphones to consider: USB and XLR.

USB microphones are ideal for beginners because of their simplicity. They plug directly into your computer, making them easy to set up and use. If you're just starting out or working with a tight budget, a USB mic like the Samson Q2U or Blue Yeti is a great choice. These microphones deliver impressive audio q...

On the other hand, XLR microphones are designed for more advanced setups. They offer greater flexibility and superior sound quality, making them the go-to choice for seasoned podcasters or those looking to take their show to the next level. However, XLR mics require an audio interface or mixer to connect to your computer, which adds to the cost and complexity. For those ready to invest, models like the Shure SM7B are industry favorites, offering crisp, professional-grade audio.

Beyond the microphone, headphones are another essential tool. They allow you to monitor your audio as you record, helping you catch issues like background noise or inconsistent volume levels. While you don't need studio-grade headphones to get started, it's worth investing in a pair that's comfortable and reliable. Options like the Audio-Technica ATH-M20x are affordable and deliver clear sound. For higher-end options, the Sony MDR-7506 is a popular choice among podcasters and audio professionals.

Once you have a microphone and headphones, consider your recording software. Programs like Audacity (free) and GarageBand (free for Mac users) are beginner-friendly and provide the basic tools you need to record and edit episodes. If you're ready to explore advanced features, paid software like Adobe Audition or Logic Pro offers more versatility and control.

While equipment is important, your recording environment plays an equally critical role in achieving high-quality audio. A quiet, echo-free space can make even a basic microphone sound great. Bedrooms, closets, or small offices often work well because soft surfaces like carpets, curtains, and furniture absorb sound and reduce reverb. For extra soundproofing, consider adding foam panels or heavy blankets to minimize unwanted noise.

Understanding these essentials—microphones, headphones, software, and your recording space—will give you a solid foundation for your podcast. Whether you're working with a modest budget or planning a professional setup, the right tools can help you deliver a show that sounds as good as your content deserves. And as you dive deeper into podcasting, you'll discover that even small improvements in equipment and setup can make a big difference in how your audience experiences your show.

When it comes to podcasting equipment, the good news is that you don't need to spend a fortune to get started. There are excellent budget-friendly options for beginners, as well as advanced tools for those ready to take their podcast to the next level. The most important thing is to choose equipment that fits your needs and helps you create a show that sounds professional and polished.

Your microphone is the cornerstone of your podcast setup, and fortunately, there's a wide range of options to suit every budget.

For beginners, USB microphones are an ideal choice. They're affordable, easy to set up, and don't require additional gear. The Samson Q2U (around $70) is often recommended for its excellent sound quality and versatility. It offers both USB and XLR connections, making it a great starter mic that you can continue using as your setup evolves. Another popular option is the Blue Yeti (around $100), known for its clear audio and fle...

If you're ready to invest in advanced equipment, consider upgrading to an XLR microphone. The Audio-Technica AT2020 (around $100) is a fantastic entry point into the XLR world, offering rich sound quality at an accessible price. For podcasters aiming for professional-grade audio, the Shure SM7B (around $400) is a gold standard. Used by top podcasters and broadcasters, it delivers exceptional clarity and reduces background noise. Keep in mind that XLR mics require an audio interface, like the **Foc...

Headphones are another essential piece of your setup, allowing you to monitor your audio in real-time and catch issues before they become problems. For budget-conscious creators, the Audio-Technica ATH-M20x (around $50) offers reliable sound and comfort at an affordable price. These headphones are lightweight and durable, making them perfect for extended recording sessions.

For podcasters seeking a higher-end option, the Sony MDR-7506 (around $100) is a favorite among audio professionals. Known for their exceptional clarity and balanced sound profile, these headphones let you hear every detail in your recording. The difference may not be immediately noticeable to beginners, but for advanced users, they're a worthy investment.

If you're using an XLR microphone, you'll need an audio interface to connect it to your computer. Budget-friendly options like the Focusrite Scarlett 2i2 (around $170) are reliable and user-friendly, providing excellent sound quality. For those who want more control over their audio, a mixer like the RODECaster Pro (around $600) adds advanced features such as sound effects, multi-channel recording, and live streaming capabilities.

While an audio interface or mixer can significantly enhance your setup, it's important to choose one that matches your level of expertise. Beginners can start with simple interfaces, while more experienced podcasters may benefit from the additional flexibility of a mixer.

Your recording software, or DAW (Digital Audio Workstation), is where you'll capture and edit your episodes. For beginners, free programs like Audacity (compatible with Windows, Mac, and Linux) or GarageBand (for Mac users) are excellent starting points. They provide all the basic tools you need to record, cut, and refine your audio.

If you're looking for more advanced features, premium software like Adobe Audition (around $20/month) or Logic Pro (a one-time purchase of $199) offers greater flexibility and precision. These tools are ideal for podcasters who want to explore multi-track editing, advanced effects, or seamless integration with other software.

Even with the best equipment, a poor recording environment can compromise the quality of your podcast. The good news? You don't need a professional studio to achieve clean, professional-sounding audio. With a few thoughtful adjustments, almost any room in your home can become a podcasting-friendly space that enhances your sound quality.

The first step is selecting the right space. Look for a room that's quiet, enclosed, and free from distractions. Bedrooms, closets, or small home offices often work well because they tend to have soft furnishings like carpets, curtains, and upholstered furniture that naturally absorb sound. These materials help minimize echo and prevent sound from bouncing off hard surfaces, which can create a hollow or "boomy" quality in your recordings.

If possible, avoid large, open spaces with lots of bare walls or hard flooring. Kitchens, living rooms with high ceilings, or rooms with tiled floors might amplify unwanted echoes and reverb. A cozy, smaller room with plenty of fabric and texture will usually give you better results.

Background noise is one of the biggest challenges in home recording. Even subtle sounds, like a humming refrigerator or a ticking clock, can be picked up by sensitive microphones and distract from your voice. Before recording, take a moment to eliminate as much noise as possible. Turn off any appliances that don't need to be running, like fans, air conditioners, or even computer notifications. Let others in your household know that you're recording and ask them to keep noise to a minimum during your ses...

Timing can also make a big difference. Pay attention to when your environment is at its quietest. Maybe the early morning hours are peaceful, or perhaps the middle of the day works best when neighbors are out and about. Scheduling your recording sessions during these quieter times can save you time and effort in post-production editing.

Soundproofing doesn't have to mean expensive renovations or professional-grade materials. Simple adjustments can significantly improve your recording environment. Start by adding soft materials to your space. Rugs, thick curtains, and pillows can all help dampen sound and reduce echo. If your room still feels too "live," try placing blankets over doors or windows to block noise from outside.

For a more polished solution, consider acoustic foam panels. These lightweight panels are affordable and easy to install on walls, ceilings, or even desktops. While you don't need to cover every inch of your room, strategically placing foam panels behind and around your recording area can make a noticeable difference in sound quality.

One creative (and cost-effective) trick is to record in a closet. Clothes hanging on racks provide excellent sound absorption, and the enclosed space naturally blocks out much of the ambient noise from the rest of your home. It might not feel glamorous, but the results often rival those of professional studios.

How you position your microphone is just as important as the type of mic you use. A common mistake is speaking too close or too far from the mic, which can lead to distortion or a loss of clarity. For most microphones, the ideal distance is about 6–12 inches from your mouth. This range captures your voice clearly without overwhelming the mic with plosive sounds (like the harsh bursts of air from "p" and "b" sounds).

To further reduce plosives, consider using a pop filter. This simple attachment sits in front of your microphone and diffuses the bursts of air from your speech, creating a smoother, cleaner sound. Another option is a foam cover, which can also help reduce wind noise and soften harsh tones.

Experiment with angling the microphone slightly off-center rather than pointing it directly at your mouth. This positioning can help reduce sharp sibilance (the hissing sound on "s" and "sh" sounds) and create a more natural tone.

While sound quality is the primary focus, don't overlook the importance of comfort and atmosphere in your recording space. A clutter-free, well-lit environment can help you feel more relaxed and confident while recording. Arrange your space so that everything you need—your microphone, headphones, notes, or laptop—is within easy reach. If you're comfortable, it will come through in your voice, making your delivery more natural and engaging.

Lighting might not seem relevant to podcasting, but it can impact your mindset. A dim, poorly lit space can feel stifling, while natural light or soft ambient lighting can create a more positive atmosphere. If you're filming video alongside your audio recordings, proper lighting will also enhance the visual quality of your content.

When you're just starting, don't stress about creating the perfect environment. Focus on making small, effective changes that fit within your budget and circumstances. The goal is to create a space where you can consistently record high-quality audio without distractions or unnecessary complications.

As your podcast grows, you'll naturally find opportunities to upgrade your space. You might invest in additional soundproofing, a professional desk setup, or even a dedicated recording room. But remember, the most important thing is to start where you are and keep improving as you go. With creativity and a little effort, you can transform any space into a podcasting haven that helps you sound your best.

The most important thing is to start. Great content and authentic storytelling matter more than expensive gear. With the right combination of tools, creativity, and determination, you can create a podcast that sounds professional and connects with your audience.

Starting a podcast can feel overwhelming, especially when faced with the seemingly endless array of equipment, software, and technical jargon. It's easy to fall into the trap of thinking you need the perfect setup or the latest gear before you hit "record." But here's the truth: your podcast's success doesn't hinge on expensive equipment or a state-of-the-art studio—it hinges on the quality of your content and the authenticity of your voice.

Some of the most popular podcasts in the world began with modest setups. Their creators didn't wait for the "perfect" microphone or spend months mastering advanced audio techniques. They started with what they had, focused on delivering value to their audience, and improved along the way. *Side Hustle School*, for instance, started with a simple mic and a clear purpose: to share actionable ideas for creating additional income. Its simplicity didn't hold it back—it became part of its charm.

The reality is that listeners care far more about your message than the slight imperfections in your sound. A compelling story, a fresh perspective, or a meaningful connection will keep your audience coming back, even if your first episodes aren't perfectly polished. People are drawn to authenticity, not perfection. If your passion shines through, your listeners will forgive minor hiccups in your production quality.

That's not to say equipment and sound quality don't matter—they do. But they're secondary to creating content that resonates. As you grow as a podcaster, you'll naturally learn ways to improve your setup and refine your production process. Upgrading your gear or experimenting with new techniques can enhance your show, but it's not a requirement to get started. Progress is more important than perfection, and the most significant leap you'll ever make is recording your first episode.

Podcasting is an iterative journey. Your first episodes will likely feel rough around the edges, and that's okay. Every podcaster, no matter how experienced, started as a beginner. The key is to embrace the learning curve and trust that you'll improve over time. With each episode, you'll gain confidence, refine your voice, and discover what works best for you and your audience.

Remember, your podcast is ultimately a reflection of you—your passions, your expertise, and your unique perspective. That's what will set you apart, not the brand of microphone you use or the size of your recording space. So, don't let technical hurdles hold you back. Start where you are, use what you have, and focus on creating something meaningful. The rest will follow.

Your audience is out there, waiting to hear what you have to say. They're not expecting perfection; they're expecting connection. And the only way to build that connection is to begin. Hit record, share your voice, and trust that your authenticity will carry you further than any piece of equipment ever could.

Chapter 6: Recording and Editing Your First Episode

There's a unique thrill that comes with preparing to record your first podcast episode. It's the moment where your ideas start to transform into something tangible, something real. But let's be honest—this stage can also feel a bit daunting. You're stepping into unfamiliar territory, and the weight of wanting everything to be perfect can sometimes overshadow the excitement of starting. Here's the good news: your first episode doesn't need to be flawless. It just needs to exist.

The key to a successful first recording is preparation. Just as an artist sketches before painting, or a writer drafts before publishing, preparing your episode helps you feel confident and ensures your recording session flows smoothly. The goal isn't to script every word (unless that's your style) but to have a roadmap that keeps you focused and organized.

Begin by outlining your episode. Think of this as a guide for your conversation or monologue. What are the key points you want to cover? What's the main takeaway you want your listeners to have? A good outline breaks your episode into manageable sections:

- **Introduction:** How will you introduce the episode? Will you open with a personal anecdote, an intriguing statistic, or a bold question? This sets the tone and grabs your listeners' attention.
- **Main Content:** What's the core of your episode? This is where you'll deliver the value—whether it's tips, a story, or a discussion. Break this section into smaller points or segments to keep it organized.
- **Conclusion:** How will you wrap up? Recap the main points, offer a call to action, or leave your listeners with a memorable takeaway.

Outlining helps you avoid rambling and ensures you hit all the points you want to cover. It's also a useful tool for editing later—you'll know exactly where each section starts and ends, making it easier to trim or adjust as needed.

For some podcasters, scripting part or all of the episode is helpful, especially if you're nervous about what to say. A script can keep you on track, minimize filler words, and ensure you deliver your message clearly. However, reading from a script word-for-word can sometimes make your delivery sound stiff or unnatural.

A good compromise is to script key sections, like your introduction or conclusion, and use bullet points or short notes for the rest. This approach allows you to stay focused while leaving room for spontaneity. Remember, the best podcasts often feel conversational, even if they're well-planned.

Before you hit "record," take some time to practice. This doesn't mean rehearsing every word—just familiarizing yourself with your outline and testing your delivery. Speak out loud to hear how your ideas flow. If something feels awkward or clunky, tweak it.

Practicing also helps you get comfortable with your microphone and recording setup. Try recording a short test segment and playing it back. How does your voice sound? Are you speaking too quickly or too slowly? Is the microphone picking up unwanted background noise? These small adjustments can make a big difference when it's time for the real recording.

Your environment plays a significant role in the quality of your recording. Choose a quiet, enclosed space with minimal background noise. Soft furnishings like carpets, curtains, and cushions can help absorb sound and reduce echo. If you're working with a budget, recording in a closet surrounded by clothes is a surprisingly effective DIY solution.

Before recording, eliminate potential distractions. Turn off fans, air conditioners, or appliances that hum. Silence your phone and close unnecessary apps on your computer to avoid notifications. Let others in your household know you'll be recording to minimize interruptions.

Test your equipment before you begin. Is your microphone positioned correctly—about 6–12 inches from your mouth and slightly off-center to avoid plosives? Are your headphones plugged in and functioning? Is your recording software set to the right input and output settings?

Taking a few minutes to double-check these details can save you from having to re-record due to technical issues.

When everything is ready, take a deep breath and hit record. The first few minutes might feel awkward, but that's okay—almost every podcaster experiences this. As you settle into your content, you'll find your rhythm. If you make a mistake, keep going. You can always edit later, and sometimes those small, unscripted moments add authenticity and charm to your podcast.

Remember, this is your first episode. It's not about achieving perfection—it's about taking the first step. Every podcaster you admire started right where you are now, and their first recordings likely had imperfections too. What matters most is that you're beginning.

By the end of your recording session, you'll have something real: your voice captured, your ideas shared, and your journey as a podcaster officially underway. That's worth celebrating.

Once you've recorded your first podcast episode, it's time to edit and polish it into a final product that's ready to share with the world. Editing can feel intimidating if you're new to it, but with beginner-friendly tools like Audacity and GarageBand, you'll quickly discover it's an approachable and even enjoyable process. Think of editing as the refining stage—it's where you clean up your audio, enhance its quality, and add creative touches like music or effects to make your episode shine.

Let's begin with the tools of the trade. Two popular options for beginners are Audacity (available for Windows, Mac, and Linux) and GarageBand (exclusive to Mac). Both are free, easy to learn, and powerful enough to produce professional-quality episodes.

Audacity: This open-source program has a straightforward interface that makes it accessible even if you've never edited audio before. You can download it for free and start editing immediately. Audacity offers tools for cutting, copying, and pasting segments of audio, as well as more advanced features like noise reduction and equalization.

GarageBand: Mac users will find GarageBand pre-installed on most devices. While it's often associated with music production, it's equally effective for podcast editing. Its clean layout and drag-and-drop functionality make it a great choice for beginners. Plus, it includes built-in loops and sound effects that you can use to enhance your episodes.

Choose the program that feels most intuitive to you. Both have plenty of tutorials available online, so you can find step-by-step guidance for any feature you want to explore.

Start by importing your recorded audio file into your chosen software. In Audacity, you can do this by dragging the file into the workspace or using the "File > Import" option. GarageBand works similarly—just drag the file onto a new track in your project.

Once your audio is loaded, you'll see it displayed as a waveform. This visual representation of your recording makes it easier to identify sections where you might need to make edits, such as long pauses, mistakes, or background noise.

Editing begins with cleaning up your raw audio. This step ensures your episode sounds clear and professional.

- **Remove Unnecessary Pauses or Mistakes**: As you listen to your recording, you'll likely notice moments where you paused for too long, stumbled over a word, or repeated a phrase. Use the selection tool in your software to highlight these sections and delete them. Be careful not to cut too aggressively—leave enough space for natural pacing.

- **Reduce Background Noise**: If your recording has a faint hum, static, or other unwanted sounds, both Audacity and GarageBand offer noise reduction tools. In Audacity, highlight a portion of your audio with background noise, go to "Effect > Noise Reduction," and let the program analyze it. Then, apply the reduction across your entire track. GarageBand's noise gate feature works similarly, automatically minimizing low-level background sounds.

- **Adjust Volume Levels**: Consistent volume is key to a pleasant listening experience. If certain parts of your audio are too loud or too quiet, use the volume adjustment tools to even them out. In Audacity, this might mean applying "Amplify" or "Normalize" effects. In GarageBand, you can manually adjust the volume line on your track.

- **Cut Unwanted Sounds**: Clicks, pops, or sudden plosive sounds (like the "p" or "b" sounds that hit your microphone too hard) can be distracting. Zoom in on the waveform to find these moments and either reduce their volume or cut them out entirely.

Once your audio is clean, it's time to add some creative flair. Music and effects can elevate your episode and give it a polished, professional feel.

- **Add Intro and Outro Music**: Choose music that reflects the tone of your podcast. For a motivational show, you might select something upbeat and energetic. For a storytelling podcast, softer, atmospheric music might work better. Websites like AudioJungle, Epidemic Sound, or Free Music Archive offer royalty-free tracks that you can use legally.

Import your chosen music file into your project and position it at the beginning (for your intro) or end (for your outro). Use the fade-in and fade-out tools to create smooth transitions between the music and your voice.

- **Incorporate Sound Effects**: Sound effects can add personality and help emphasize key moments. For example, you might use a subtle "ding" sound to mark transitions between segments or a drum roll before a big reveal. GarageBand comes with a library of effects you can drag and drop directly into your project.

- **Layer Tracks for Professional Sound**: Most editing software allows you to work with multiple tracks. Use one track for your voice, another for music, and additional tracks for sound effects. This separation makes it easier to adjust the timing and volume of each element individually, ensuring everything blends seamlessly.

Once you've cleaned and enhanced your audio, listen to the entire episode from start to finish. Pay attention to how it flows—do your transitions feel smooth? Are there any abrupt cuts or awkward pauses? If something feels off, go back and adjust it.

Here are some final touches to consider:

- **Equalization (EQ):** Adjust the EQ settings to make your voice sound clearer and more balanced. Many programs offer presets, like "Podcast Voice," that automatically enhance vocal frequencies.
- **Compression:** Compression evens out volume levels across your episode, ensuring that quieter parts aren't drowned out and louder sections don't overwhelm the listener. Most beginner-friendly software includes a simple compression tool with preset options.
- **Add Tags and Metadata:** Before exporting your file, add metadata like the episode title, description, and podcast name. This information will display in podcast directories when your episode is published.

Finally, export your edited episode as an MP3 file. Most hosting platforms recommend a bit rate of 128 kbps or higher for good audio quality. Save a copy of your project file as well, in case you need to revisit or revise it later.

Editing doesn't have to be intimidating. With tools like Audacity and GarageBand, you have everything you need to turn your raw recording into a polished podcast episode. The process may feel slow at first, but with practice, you'll develop an efficient workflow that makes editing second nature.

Remember, the goal isn't perfection—it's progress. Each episode you edit is a step toward becoming more comfortable and confident in your skills. Over time, you'll discover your personal editing style, whether it's a minimalist approach that keeps things raw and conversational or a more produced sound with music, effects, and precise cuts.

Most importantly, don't let the technical aspects of editing hold you back. Embrace the learning curve, experiment with different tools and techniques, and trust that each episode will bring you closer to mastering the craft. Editing is where your podcast starts to take shape, and it's an exciting opportunity to bring your vision to life.

Publishing your first podcast episode is a big deal. It's the culmination of your planning, preparation, and effort, and it's the moment your ideas finally take flight. But let's be honest—it's easy to get caught up in second-guessing. Is the audio quality good enough? Did I say the right things? Will anyone even listen? These doubts are natural, but they shouldn't hold you back. The truth is, no one's first episode is perfect. And that's okay—because perfection isn't the goal. Progress is.

Think about some of the world's most successful podcasters. They didn't start with flawless production or polished delivery. They started with a microphone, a story to tell, and a willingness to learn as they went. *The Tim Ferriss Show*, now one of the most downloaded podcasts in history, began with Tim experimenting, making mistakes, and finding his rhythm. Ira Glass of *This American Life* has famously said that everyone's early work is a bit of a mess—but it's part of the process.

Your first episode isn't a finished product; it's a starting point. Every podcaster begins with a gap between the vision in their head and what they can produce in the beginning. What matters is closing that gap over time through consistent effort and learning. The only way to do that is to begin.

It's tempting to obsess over every detail: trimming every pause, perfecting your transitions, or editing out every "um." But here's the thing—your listeners aren't expecting studio-level production. They're here for your voice, your perspective, and the value you bring. Authenticity matters far more than polish.

Think of your podcast like a conversation with a friend. If a friend stumbled over a word or paused to collect their thoughts, would you mind? Probably not. Those little imperfections are what make conversations real and relatable. Your podcast should feel the same way.

That doesn't mean you shouldn't aim for quality. Of course, you want your audio to be clear and your content engaging. But don't let the pursuit of perfection paralyze you. You'll improve with every episode—your delivery will get smoother, your editing faster, and your production more refined. The important thing is to start creating, even if it's not perfect yet.

Your first episode is more than just an audio file. It's a milestone—a tangible result of your effort, creativity, and courage to put yourself out there. It represents the leap from thinking about podcasting to actually doing it, and that's something to be proud of.

Take a moment to celebrate. Share your episode with friends and family, treat yourself to something special, or simply reflect on how far you've come. Acknowledging your progress isn't just about feeling good—it's about building momentum. Celebrating this first step gives you the energy and confidence to keep going.

It's easy to fall into the trap of thinking you need everything to be perfect before you launch. But the reality is, your audience isn't waiting for perfection—they're waiting for your voice. They're looking for stories, insights, or inspiration that only you can provide. By holding back, you're delaying the opportunity to connect with people who need to hear what you have to say.

Think about the podcasts you love. Chances are, you didn't start listening because they had the best production values. You stuck around because of the content, the host's personality, or the way it made you feel. Your audience will approach your podcast the same way. They care about what you're saying, not whether your intro music fades out perfectly.

Podcasting is a journey of constant learning. The things you worry about now—audio quality, pacing, delivery—will become second nature as you gain experience. Each episode you create will teach you something new, whether it's how to streamline your editing process, engage your audience, or improve your storytelling.

Mistakes are part of the process. They're how you learn, adapt, and grow as a creator. Maybe your microphone wasn't positioned perfectly, or you stumbled over a word. These moments aren't failures—they're stepping stones. By publishing your first episode, you're laying the foundation for a body of work that will evolve and improve over time.

One day, you'll look back on your first episode with a mix of nostalgia and pride. It might feel rough compared to your later work, but it will also be a reminder of how far you've come. That first episode is a snapshot of where you started—a testament to your willingness to try, learn, and grow.

The podcasters you admire didn't become great overnight. They started small, made mistakes, and improved through consistency and effort. You're on the same path. Every episode you publish brings you closer to your goals, and it all begins with the courage to hit "publish" for the first time.

So, here's your next step: take a deep breath, embrace the imperfections, and publish your first episode. Let it be a celebration of your creativity, a commitment to your goals, and a connection to the audience you're about to build.

Remember, this isn't the end of your journey—it's just the beginning. You'll grow as a podcaster, refine your craft, and create content that resonates with your audience. But none of that happens until you take the leap.

Your voice matters, your story matters, and your perspective matters. The world is ready to hear what you have to say. So go ahead—publish that first episode, celebrate the milestone, and step confidently into your podcasting journey. The best is yet to come.

Chapter 7: Hosting and Distributing Your Podcast

Creating a podcast is more than just recording and editing episodes—it's about getting those episodes into the ears of your audience. That's where hosting and distribution come into play. Think of a podcast hosting platform as the backbone of your show. It's the service that stores your audio files, generates the RSS feed for your podcast, and ensures your episodes are available on popular listening apps like Apple Podcasts, Spotify, and Google Podcasts. Without a hosting platform, your podcast wouldn't...

At its core, a podcast hosting platform is a digital home for your show. When you upload an episode, your hosting service generates a unique RSS feed. This feed acts as a bridge between your podcast and the directories where people discover and listen to shows. The RSS feed ensures that every new episode you publish is automatically updated and available to your audience, no matter which app they use.

You might wonder, "Can't I just upload my podcast directly to Apple or Spotify?" The answer is no—those platforms don't host audio files. Instead, they rely on the RSS feed generated by your hosting platform to pull in your episodes. This is why choosing a reliable hosting service is so important.

Hosting platforms come in all shapes and sizes, each offering unique features. Some, like Buzzsprout, are designed to be beginner-friendly with simple dashboards and analytics. Others, like Anchor, are free and include tools for recording and editing. Premium platforms, such as Libsyn, cater to seasoned podcasters with advanced customization options and robust storage plans. Your choice will depend on your budget, goals, and technical comfort level, but the right platform will make the process ...

Hosting platforms also play a vital role in distributing your podcast to directories. These directories—Apple Podcasts, Spotify, Google Podcasts, Amazon Music, and others—are where your audience will discover, subscribe, and listen to your show. Each directory serves as a gateway to potential listeners, and the more directories you're listed on, the broader your reach.

Podcasting has never been more accessible, thanks to hosting platforms that handle much of the technical heavy lifting. By understanding what hosting platforms do and why they matter, you'll set yourself up for success as you take the next steps toward distributing your podcast and reaching your audience. This is the stage where your podcast transforms from an idea into a shared experience—accessible to listeners around the globe.

Once your podcast is ready to launch, the next step is to make it accessible to listeners everywhere. Hosting platforms like Buzzsprout and Anchor simplify this process, guiding you from uploading your episodes to submitting them to popular directories like Apple Podcasts and Spotify. While the steps might seem technical at first glance, they're straightforward once you break them down. Let's walk through the process step by step.

Start by selecting a podcast hosting platform that fits your needs. For beginners, user-friendly platforms like Buzzsprout or Anchor are excellent choices. Buzzsprout offers a clean interface and powerful analytics to help you track your podcast's growth, while Anchor provides free hosting and integrated tools for recording and editing. More advanced podcasters may prefer platforms like Libsyn, which offers extensive customization and monetization options.

Create an account on your chosen platform and follow their setup instructions. Most platforms will ask for basic information about your podcast, such as its title, description, and category. Take your time here—this information will be visible to listeners and should reflect your podcast's identity. A clear, engaging description can make the difference between a potential listener pressing "play" or scrolling past.

Your podcast's cover art is one of the first things potential listeners will notice. It should be visually appealing, reflect your podcast's theme, and adhere to the technical specifications required by hosting platforms. Most platforms recommend a square image of at least 3000 x 3000 pixels in PNG or JPEG format.

If you haven't already created artwork, tools like Canva or Adobe Express make it easy to design professional-looking covers. Alternatively, you can hire a freelance designer through services like Fiverr or 99Designs. Once your artwork is ready, upload it to your hosting platform during the setup process.

With your account set up and your artwork in place, it's time to upload your first episode. Most hosting platforms allow you to drag and drop your audio file into their dashboard. Before uploading, ensure your file is in the correct format—usually MP3 with a bit rate of 128 kbps or higher for optimal sound quality.

After uploading, you'll be prompted to fill in metadata for the episode. This includes:

- **Episode Title:** Make it descriptive and intriguing. A title like "How to Stay Productive When You're Overwhelmed" is more enticing than "Episode 1."
- **Episode Description:** Provide a short summary of the episode's content. Include keywords to help with discoverability and any relevant links or resources mentioned in the episode.

- **Episode Number:** Numbering your episodes helps listeners follow along, especially if your content builds sequentially.
- **Release Date and Time:** You can publish immediately or schedule the episode for a specific date and time.

Once your episode is uploaded, your hosting platform will generate an RSS feed for your podcast. This feed is a unique URL that acts as the connection between your hosting platform and podcast directories. Every time you publish a new episode, the directories pull the update from your RSS feed, ensuring your content stays current across all platforms.

Copy your RSS feed URL—it's the key to submitting your podcast to directories.

Now it's time to distribute your podcast to the directories where listeners will find and subscribe to your show. Each directory has its own submission process, but the general steps are similar.

1. Apple Podcasts

Apple Podcasts is one of the largest directories and a must for most podcasters. Here's how to get listed:

- Visit [Apple Podcasts Connect](#) and sign in with your Apple ID.
- Click the "+" button to add a new show.
- Paste your RSS feed URL and click "Validate." This checks that your feed is correctly formatted.
- Review the preview to ensure your podcast details are accurate.
- Submit your podcast for approval. Apple's review process can take anywhere from a few hours to a few days. You'll receive an email once your show is approved.

2. Spotify

Spotify is another major player in podcast distribution, with a growing listener base. Submitting to Spotify is straightforward:

- Log in to your hosting platform. Many platforms, like Buzzsprout, include a built-in option to submit directly to Spotify.
- If your hosting platform doesn't have this feature, visit [Spotify for Podcasters](#).
- Log in with your Spotify account or create one if you don't have one.
- Click "Get Started" and paste your RSS feed URL.
- Review your podcast details and submit. Spotify typically lists new shows within 24 hours.

3. Google Podcasts

Google Podcasts is essential for Android users. Here's how to get listed:

- Visit the Google Podcasts Manager and sign in with your Google account.
- Paste your RSS feed URL and click "Next."
- Verify ownership of your podcast by following the instructions (usually sending a verification code to your email).
- Submit your podcast for indexing.

After submitting to the big three (Apple, Spotify, and Google), consider additional directories like Amazon Music, Stitcher, iHeartRadio, and TuneIn Many hosting platforms offer easy integrations, allowing you to distribute to multiple directories with just a few clicks.

Once your podcast is listed in directories, you're ready to launch! Share your show on social media, email it to friends and family, and include links in blog posts or newsletters. Encourage listeners to subscribe, leave reviews, and share your episodes with others.

Don't forget to monitor your hosting platform's analytics. Insights like download numbers, listener demographics, and popular episodes can help you refine your content and grow your audience.

Distributing your podcast might feel like a big step, but hosting platforms make the process surprisingly simple. By following these steps, you'll ensure that your show is available wherever listeners are searching for new content. And once it's out there, the real fun begins—connecting with your audience and sharing your voice with the world.

Getting your podcast onto directories is a huge milestone, but it's only the first step in building your audience. To truly stand out in the crowded world of podcasting, you need to focus on the details that help listeners find, understand, and connect with your show. This is where metadata, show notes, and descriptions play a vital role.

Metadata is the digital foundation of your podcast—it's the information that tells directories and search engines what your show is about. Every time someone searches for a podcast on a specific topic, the metadata determines whether your show appears in the results. Without well-crafted metadata, even the most engaging podcast can remain invisible to potential listeners.

Start with your podcast title. It should be concise, specific, and reflective of your content. If your title is too vague, like *The Weekly Show*, it won't stand out in searches. On the other hand, something descriptive like *Side Hustle Stories: Real-Life Tips for Entrepreneurs* not only grabs attention but also makes it clear who your podcast is for.

Next, focus on your podcast description. Think of this as your elevator pitch—a few sentences that explain what your show is about and why listeners should care. Use keywords strategically, but don't sacrifice clarity for the sake of cramming in terms. A good description doesn't just inform; it invites. For example:

"Welcome to *Wellness Unpacked*, the podcast that simplifies health and wellness so you can build habits that stick. Each week, we share practical tips, expert insights, and inspiring stories to help you live your best life—without the overwhelm."

This description not only tells potential listeners what to expect but also makes an emotional connection by addressing a common pain point (feeling overwhelmed by wellness advice).

Show notes are another essential tool for attracting and retaining listeners. Think of them as the written companion to your episodes, providing a roadmap of the content and a gateway to additional resources. When done right, show notes can boost your podcast's search engine optimization (SEO), helping new listeners discover your episodes through Google and other search engines.

Each set of show notes should include:

- **An Episode Summary:** Highlight the main topics covered in the episode. This gives listeners a quick overview of what they'll learn or enjoy by tuning in.
- **Key Takeaways or Bullet Points:** Break down the episode into digestible points. For example, "In this episode, we discuss: 1) How to stay productive while working remotely, 2) Tools for effective time management, 3) Overcoming common remote work challenges."
- **Links to Resources:** Include links to websites, articles, or tools mentioned in the episode. This adds value for listeners and positions you as a trusted source of information.
- **Guest Information:** If your episode features a guest, share their bio, links to their work, and where listeners can connect with them online.
- **A Call to Action:** Encourage listeners to subscribe, leave a review, or follow you on social media. Clear, direct calls to action are more effective than vague requests like "Check out our website."

Well-crafted show notes are a powerful way to extend the life of your episodes. They provide a bridge between your audio content and your listeners' broader experience, making your podcast more engaging and shareable.

Episode descriptions are your chance to hook potential listeners as they browse through directories. Unlike your show notes, which live on your website or hosting platform, descriptions appear directly in apps like Apple Podcasts and Spotify. They need to be short, punchy, and intriguing—typically no more than a few sentences.

The best descriptions balance clarity with curiosity. For example, instead of writing:

"This episode talks about managing stress."

Try something more specific and engaging:

"Feeling overwhelmed? In this episode, we share three simple techniques to reduce stress and regain your focus—no meditation app required."

Adding a touch of personality and speaking directly to the listener's needs can make your descriptions stand out. Remember, people are scanning quickly, so your words need to grab attention in an instant.

One of the most overlooked aspects of optimizing your podcast is maintaining consistency across all platforms. Your title, artwork, and descriptions should match wherever your podcast appears. Inconsistent branding can confuse potential listeners or make your show look less professional. When everything aligns, you create a cohesive identity that helps people remember and trust your podcast.

Consistency also applies to how you format your metadata and show notes. If listeners know they can count on you for detailed show notes, actionable takeaways, or direct links to resources, they're more likely to subscribe and stick around. Over time, these small details build loyalty.

Optimization isn't a one-time task—it's an ongoing process. As you release more episodes, take note of what resonates with your audience. Which keywords or topics drive the most traffic? Are there specific formats or phrases that consistently perform well? Use analytics from your hosting platform to refine your metadata and descriptions.

Additionally, don't be afraid to revisit and update old episodes. If you've improved your writing style or identified better keywords, go back and polish earlier descriptions and show notes. This not only makes your archive more appealing to new listeners but can also improve your podcast's discoverability over time.

While optimizing metadata, show notes, and descriptions is crucial, it's important to remember that none of these tactics will matter without great content. Think of optimization as a way to enhance and amplify your message—not replace it. A beautifully written description won't save a dull episode, but it *will* help an engaging one reach more listeners.

Your goal is to make it as easy as possible for people to find, understand, and connect with your podcast. Metadata and descriptions open the door, but it's your voice, stories, and insights that keep them coming back.

Podcasting is about building relationships. Every piece of metadata, every episode description, and every line of show notes is a chance to deepen your connection with your audience. By taking the time to optimize these details, you're not just attracting listeners—you're inviting them into a conversation that's meaningful, engaging, and uniquely yours.

Whether you're just starting or looking to grow your podcast, remember: every word matters. Use them wisely, and they'll guide your audience straight to you.

Chapter 8: Monetizing Your Podcast

For many podcasters, the idea of turning a passion project into a source of income is both exciting and daunting. Podcasting offers a variety of monetization opportunities, from securing sponsorships to selling merchandise. The good news? You don't need millions of downloads to start making money. What you do need is a clear understanding of your options, realistic expectations, and a commitment to building value for your audience.

At its core, podcast monetization is about creating a win-win situation. You deliver content that your listeners love, and in return, they support you—whether through their wallets, by engaging with your sponsors, or by purchasing something you've created. This relationship is built on trust, so your first priority should always be producing high-quality episodes that resonate with your audience. Once you've established that connection, monetization becomes a natural extension of the value you're already providing.

Let's start by exploring the most common ways podcasters generate income.

Sponsorships are one of the most well-known ways to monetize a podcast. In this model, companies pay you to promote their products or services during your episodes. You've probably heard podcasters say things like, "This episode is brought to you by…" followed by a brief ad. That's a sponsorship.

For beginner podcasters, landing a sponsorship might feel like a distant goal, but it's not as out of reach as you might think. Many companies are interested in niche audiences, and even small podcasts can be valuable if they have engaged listeners. Sponsors typically pay based on your number of downloads, but some may also consider factors like your niche, audience demographics, or the quality of your content.

A typical sponsorship deal involves agreeing on an ad type (pre-roll, mid-roll, or post-roll) and a payment model. Cost per mille (CPM) is the most common model, where sponsors pay a set amount for every 1,000 downloads. For example, if a sponsor offers $25 CPM and your episode gets 5,000 downloads, you'd earn $125. While this might not sound like much at first, it can add up as your audience grows.

Crowdfunding allows your audience to support your podcast directly. Platforms like Patreon, Ko-fi, and Buy Me a Coffee make it easy to set up a system where listeners can contribute a few dollars per month or make one-time donations. In return, you can offer perks like bonus episodes, ad-free content, or behind-the-scenes updates.

Crowdfunding works best when you have a loyal and engaged audience. It's not about asking for charity—it's about offering listeners an opportunity to invest in content they value. Many podcasters find that even a small percentage of their audience is willing to contribute, especially if they feel like they're part of a community.

Take the podcast *Lore*, for example. Host Aaron Mahnke started offering bonus episodes and early access to subscribers on Patreon, and the support he received helped him turn his hobby into a full-time career. Crowdfunding is a flexible option that can grow alongside your podcast, allowing you to scale the rewards you offer as your audience expands.

Selling merchandise is another popular monetization strategy, especially for podcasts with a strong brand or dedicated following. From T-shirts and mugs to stickers and tote bags, merch gives your listeners a tangible way to support your show and spread the word.

The key to successful merchandise is creating items that resonate with your audience. For example, if your podcast has a catchy tagline, turning it into a graphic design for a T-shirt can be a hit. Tools like Teespring, Printful, or Shopify make it easy to design and sell products without needing to manage inventory or handle shipping.

Merch isn't just about profit—it's also about branding. Every time a listener wears your T-shirt or uses your mug, they're helping promote your podcast. While it might take time to see significant income from merchandise, it's a fun and creative way to engage with your audience and build your brand's visibility.

These strategies—sponsorships, crowdfunding, and merchandise—are just the beginning. From offering premium content to creating online courses or hosting live events, the possibilities for monetizing your podcast are as diverse as the content you create. The key is to choose the strategies that align with your audience, goals, and style. In the next section, we'll dive into how to set realistic expectations and build the foundation for long-term success.

When podcasters dream of monetization, it's easy to imagine sponsorship deals rolling in or merchandise flying off the shelves. But the reality is that making money from your podcast takes time, patience, and a solid foundation of listeners. Before you focus on income, it's crucial to focus on your audience. Without a dedicated listener base, even the most creative monetization strategies won't gain traction.

While every podcast's journey is unique, there are some common stages to building a show that generates income.

- **The Launch Phase (0–3 Months):**

1. Your first goal as a podcaster is to find your voice and establish your content. This stage is all about consistency—releasing episodes on a regular schedule, refining your format, and figuring out what resonates with your audience. Your listener count may start small, and that's perfectly fine. Focus on delivering value to those who are tuning in and encouraging them to share your podcast.

- **The Growth Phase (3–12 Months):**

As you release more episodes, your audience will begin to grow organically. Word of mouth, social media promotion, and being listed in podcast directories like Apple Podcasts and Spotify will help new listeners discover your show. During this phase, you might experiment with small-scale monetization, such as setting up a Patreon or adding affiliate links to your show notes. However, most of your energy should remain on producing quality content and deepening your connection with your audience.

- **The Monetization Phase (12+ Months):**

By the one-year mark, many podcasts have built enough momentum to start exploring more robust monetization strategies. This might include sponsorship deals, selling merchandise, or offering premium content. By now, you'll have a clearer sense of what your audience values and which strategies are a good fit for your show.

One of the best examples of audience-first podcasting is *Crime Junkie*, a true-crime show hosted by Ashley Flowers and Brit Prawat. When the podcast launched in 2017, it didn't start with sponsorships or merchandise. Instead, the hosts focused on creating engaging, high-quality episodes that resonated with true-crime fans.

Their approach paid off. Over time, *Crime Junkie* gained a loyal following through word of mouth and social media. Once the show had established its audience, monetization followed naturally. Today, *Crime Junkie* generates significant revenue through sponsorships, a robust Patreon community, and exclusive merchandise—but none of that would have been possible without the solid listener base they built first.

The lesson here is clear: the best monetization strategies are built on a foundation of trust and value. Listeners need to feel connected to your content before they're willing to support it financially.

Growing an audience isn't just about increasing download numbers; it's about creating a community. Your listeners are more than just statistics—they're people who choose to spend their time with your podcast. Treating them as such is one of the most powerful things you can do to build loyalty and, eventually, monetize effectively.

Start by engaging with your audience on multiple levels. Respond to their comments on social media, encourage them to email or message you with feedback, and ask for their input on future episodes. For example, if you host a wellness podcast, you might ask listeners to share their biggest health challenges, then create an episode addressing those topics. This kind of interaction not only builds trust but also gives you valuable insight into what your audience cares about.

Joshua Fields Millburn and Ryan Nicodemus, hosts of *The Minimalists Podcast*, took audience engagement to a whole new level. They started their podcast as an extension of their blog, using it to share insights about living a meaningful life with less. From the beginning, they encouraged listener participation, often answering questions or addressing topics suggested by their audience.

This focus on community allowed *The Minimalists Podcast* to grow steadily over time. Today, the show generates income through speaking engagements, book sales, and exclusive content on Patreon. Their story highlights the importance of creating value first and building relationships with your listeners before focusing on income.

One of the biggest misconceptions about podcasting is that it's a quick path to income. While some shows do achieve rapid success, the vast majority follow a slower, more organic trajectory. And that's not a bad thing—it gives you time to refine your content, experiment with your format, and truly understand your audience's needs.

Be realistic about your goals. If your podcast attracts a few hundred dedicated listeners within the first six months, that's an achievement worth celebrating. Sponsorships and other monetization strategies often come into play as your audience grows, but it's okay to start small. Even modest streams of income, like a handful of Patreon supporters or a few affiliate sales, can be encouraging milestones.

Podcasting success often follows a snowball effect. As your audience grows, your ability to monetize increases—and as you start monetizing, your resources expand, allowing you to improve your content and reach even more listeners.

Consider how podcaster Pat Flynn built his brand. He started small with *The Smart Passive Income Podcast*, focusing on delivering actionable advice for entrepreneurs. Over time, his audience grew, and he began incorporating monetization strategies like affiliate marketing and sponsorships. Today, his podcast is a cornerstone of a thriving business empire.

The takeaway? Building an audience first isn't just a step in the process—it's the foundation for everything that follows.

As you think about monetizing your podcast, keep this in mind: your listeners are your greatest asset. Sponsorships, merchandise, and crowdfunding all rely on a strong connection with your audience. If you focus on delivering consistent value—whether that's through education, entertainment, or inspiration—the income will follow naturally.

Monetization isn't the finish line; it's part of the journey. By putting your audience first and taking the time to grow your podcast authentically, you'll set yourself up for long-term success—and build a community of listeners who are as invested in your podcast as you are.

Monetizing your podcast can feel like the ultimate goal—the moment where your hard work pays off and your passion becomes a sustainable venture. But in reality, monetization is just one piece of the podcasting journey, and it's a piece that works best when it's built on a strong foundation of high-quality content and a loyal audience. The most successful podcasters don't focus on monetization as their primary aim; they focus on creating value. When you prioritize delivering consistent, engaging content, monetization becomes a natural and sustainable outcome.

It's important to approach monetization with the right mindset. Think of it as a marathon, not a sprint. Overnight success stories are rare, but incremental growth is attainable and far more reliable. By setting realistic expectations and focusing on building a solid base, you position yourself for long-term success.

Many podcasters begin with a small audience and limited resources, but they invest their energy in understanding their listeners and delivering content that resonates. As their audience grows, opportunities for monetization naturally follow. Whether it's landing a sponsorship deal, launching a Patreon, or selling merchandise, these steps feel less daunting when they're grounded in a strong connection with your listeners.

At its heart, podcasting is about connection. Your audience chooses to spend their time with you because they find value in what you offer—whether it's education, entertainment, inspiration, or a mix of all three. That connection is built through consistent, high-quality content. It's the cornerstone of your podcast and the foundation for any monetization strategy.

Listeners are savvy. They can tell when a podcast prioritizes revenue over value, and they'll respond accordingly. By focusing on your content first, you're not just creating episodes; you're building trust. And trust is what turns casual listeners into loyal fans—and eventually, supporters of your podcast through sponsorships, crowdfunding, or purchases.

It's easy to get caught up in short-term goals, like securing your first sponsor or hitting a revenue milestone. But the most successful podcasters play the long game. They recognize that sustainable monetization is built on a foundation of quality, consistency, and audience engagement.

Take a moment to reflect on why you started your podcast. Chances are, it wasn't just to make money. Maybe you wanted to share your expertise, tell stories that matter, or connect with like-minded people. Those original goals are what will keep you motivated when challenges arise, and they're also what will draw listeners to your show.

Monetization should enhance your podcast, not overshadow it. Think of it as a way to support your creative vision and expand your reach. Whether that means reinvesting in better equipment, hiring a team to help with production, or freeing up time to focus on content creation, monetization is a tool—not the endgame.

Look to the podcasters you admire, and you'll see a common theme: they all started small. Before they had sponsors or merchandise, they had passion and a commitment to creating something meaningful. Over time, their dedication paid off—not because they chased monetization, but because they built something worth supporting.

Stuff You Should Know, for example, began as a simple educational podcast. Hosts Josh and Chuck focused on delivering fascinating, well-researched episodes, and their audience grew organically. Sponsorships and other monetization opportunities followed, but the heart of their podcast—high-quality, engaging content—remained the same.

Their story isn't unique. Whether it's *The Minimalists, Crime Junkie,* or *How I Built This,* the podcasters who thrive are those who stay true to their purpose and let monetization grow naturally out of their audience's trust and support.

It's easy to fixate on big milestones, like reaching a certain number of downloads or landing a sponsorship. But don't overlook the smaller victories along the way. Every episode you publish, every new listener you gain, and every piece of feedback you receive is a step forward.

Celebrate these moments—they're proof that your podcast is making an impact. And as you continue to grow, you'll find that these small wins add up to something much bigger.

At the end of the day, monetization is just one part of your podcasting journey. What truly matters is the impact you're making—the stories you're telling, the ideas you're sharing, and the connections you're building. Your voice matters, and your audience is listening because they value what you have to say.

When you prioritize quality, authenticity, and value, monetization will come. It might take time, but the rewards will be well worth the wait—not just in terms of revenue, but in the fulfillment of knowing you've created something meaningful.

So, keep showing up. Keep creating. And trust that the work you're doing now is laying the groundwork for something incredible. The road to monetization is a long one, but with patience, persistence, and a focus on quality, you're already on your way.

Chapter 9: Marketing and Growing Your Audience

Starting a podcast is an act of creativity, but growing your audience is a strategic endeavor. While the thrill of launching your first episode is unforgettable, what comes next often presents the real challenge: getting people to listen. In a world where thousands of new podcasts are launched every month, standing out can feel like an uphill battle. But with the right approach, gaining listeners isn't just possible—it's entirely achievable.

Here's the first reality check: no matter how good your content is, listeners won't magically appear. Building an audience takes time, effort, and consistent promotion. It's not enough to create great episodes; you have to actively share them with the world. Think of marketing as an extension of your podcast, a way to amplify your voice and connect with people who will genuinely value what you're offering.

The challenge of growing a podcast isn't unique to beginners. Even seasoned podcasters face hurdles in expanding their reach. But what separates those who succeed from those who struggle is a willingness to embrace the process and experiment with different strategies. Some efforts might not yield immediate results, and that's okay—what matters is staying consistent and learning what works for your unique audience.

Imagine subscribing to a magazine only to have issues arrive sporadically—sometimes three in a month, sometimes none for half a year. You'd likely lose interest, even if the content was good. The same principle applies to podcasts. Consistency isn't just about when you release episodes; it's about showing up reliably for your audience, building a routine that they can count on.

Your listeners need to know when to expect new content. Whether you release episodes weekly, biweekly, or monthly, choose a schedule that works for you and stick to it. Over time, this regularity creates a rhythm that your audience comes to anticipate, making your podcast a consistent part of their lives.

Think about your favorite podcasts. Chances are, you know when new episodes drop and plan your listening accordingly. That predictability strengthens the relationship between you and your audience, fostering a sense of trust. They'll begin to see your podcast as a dependable source of value.

Consistency isn't just about timing; it's about maintaining a high standard for your content. Every episode should feel intentional and thoughtfully produced. This doesn't mean every detail has to be perfect—authenticity often resonates more than polish—but your audience should feel that you care about delivering value each time.

For example, if your podcast is known for actionable advice, ensure every episode delivers on that promise. If storytelling is your strength, maintain the same level of narrative depth that your listeners expect. When your audience knows they'll consistently get something worthwhile, they'll keep coming back.

Life happens, and there will inevitably be times when sticking to your schedule feels challenging. That's why planning ahead is crucial. Batch-recording episodes or having a few "evergreen" episodes in reserve can help you maintain consistency during busy periods. This way, even if unexpected events disrupt your routine, your audience won't notice a gap in your content.

While consistency gets listeners to show up, it's value that makes them stay. Your podcast should serve as more than just background noise—it should enrich your audience's lives in some way. Whether that value comes from making them laugh, teaching them something new, or inspiring them to take action, it's the driving force behind their loyalty.

What sets your podcast apart from the thousands of others in your niche? Is it your storytelling style, your expertise, or your unique perspective? Defining this value proposition helps you stay focused and ensures that every episode delivers on your podcast's core promise.

For instance, a personal finance podcast might focus on actionable advice for beginners, while another might cater to seasoned investors with in-depth market analysis. Both offer value, but their audiences are drawn to them for different reasons. Understanding your specific value helps you craft content that resonates deeply with your target listeners.

The most successful podcasters keep their listeners' needs and interests at the forefront. Think of your audience as partners in your podcasting journey. What are they struggling with? What topics do they want to learn about? The more you tailor your content to their preferences, the more valuable your podcast becomes.

Consider engaging directly with your audience to find out what they want. You can use social media polls, email newsletters, or even questions at the end of your episodes to invite feedback. For example:

- "What topics would you like me to cover next?"
- "Did this episode resonate with you? Let me know!"

This engagement not only helps you refine your content but also strengthens the bond with your listeners, making them feel heard and valued.

Every episode should leave your audience with something—an insight, a new perspective, or even just a good laugh. Think of each episode as a mini journey:

- **Start Strong:** Grab their attention with a compelling intro that sets the stage.
- **Deliver Value:** Dive into the heart of your topic with clear, actionable points or engaging storytelling.
- **End Memorable:** Leave them with a call to action, a thought-provoking question, or a takeaway that lingers in their minds.

Listeners are more likely to recommend your podcast to others when they feel like they've gained something valuable. This word-of-mouth marketing is one of the most powerful tools for growing your audience.

Consistency and value aren't separate goals—they work hand in hand. Consistency builds the foundation of trust that keeps listeners coming back, while value strengthens that trust and turns casual listeners into dedicated fans. Together, they create a virtuous cycle:

- **Consistency ensures your audience knows when to tune in.**
- **Value ensures they'll keep tuning in.**
- **Together, they make your podcast something listeners look forward to and share with others.**

For example, consider the podcast *Stuff You Should Know*. It releases episodes consistently, offering deep dives into fascinating topics. Listeners trust the schedule and know they'll always walk away having learned something new. That combination of reliability and value has turned *Stuff You Should Know* into one of the most beloved podcasts in the world.

By prioritizing consistency and value, you're not just creating a podcast—you're building a relationship with your audience. Every time they press play, they're investing their time in you, and it's your job to make that investment worthwhile. With these two foundational elements in place, your podcast is primed for growth, engagement, and long-term success. From here, the marketing tactics you implement will be the icing on the cake, amplifying the trust and value you've already established.

Effective marketing starts with understanding who you're trying to reach. Who is your ideal listener? What are their interests, challenges, and habits? The more you know about your audience, the easier it is to craft messages that resonate with them.

For example, if your podcast focuses on personal finance for young professionals, your audience might be people in their 20s and 30s who are navigating student loans, first jobs, and saving for the future. With this profile in mind, you can tailor your marketing efforts to platforms and messaging that appeal to this group—like Instagram posts that highlight budgeting tips or LinkedIn articles about career growth.

It's important to acknowledge that growing a podcast audience takes patience. At first, your episodes might only reach a handful of listeners, and that can feel discouraging. But every successful podcaster has been in your shoes. *The Daily*, one of the most popular podcasts in the world, started as an experiment at *The New York Times*. Its success didn't happen overnight—it grew because the team stayed consistent and continuously refined their content to meet audience needs.

Your journey will be similar. While the path to growth may feel slow, each listener you gain is a small victory. These early adopters are often your most loyal supporters—the people who will share your podcast with their friends, leave positive reviews, and cheer you on as your audience expands.

In the next section, we'll explore specific, actionable strategies you can use to market your podcast and connect with the listeners who are waiting to discover it. For now, remember this: marketing is less about overnight success and more about showing up, engaging authentically, and staying committed to your vision. The rest will follow.

Once you've recorded and published your podcast episodes, the next step is spreading the word. Marketing your podcast effectively requires a mix of creativity, consistency, and strategic thinking. The good news is that you don't need a massive budget or a professional marketing team to see results. With the right approach, you can steadily grow your audience and make meaningful connections with your listeners. Let's break down actionable strategies that can help you promote your podcast and reach more people.

Social media platforms are some of the most effective tools for podcast promotion. They allow you to connect directly with potential listeners, share updates, and engage with your audience in real time. Here's how to maximize your efforts:

You don't need to be on every social media platform. Instead, focus on the ones where your target audience spends the most time. For example:

- **Instagram:** Great for visual content and behind-the-scenes glimpses. Ideal for lifestyle, wellness, and storytelling podcasts.
- **Twitter/X:** Excellent for engaging in trending conversations and sharing quick updates. Works well for news, tech, and opinion-driven podcasts.
- **TikTok:** Perfect for short, engaging videos. If your podcast has a humorous or relatable element, this platform can help you go viral.
- **LinkedIn:** Best for professional or educational podcasts, especially if you're targeting entrepreneurs or industry experts.

Posting links to your episodes isn't enough. Social media is all about engaging content that captures attention. Try:

- Sharing audiograms—short audio clips from your episodes paired with subtitles and visuals. Tools like Headliner make this process easy.
- Posting behind-the-scenes photos or videos of your recording process.
- Engaging with your audience through polls, Q&A sessions, or live streams.

Social media isn't a one-way street. Reply to comments, thank people who share your content, and participate in relevant conversations. Building a community around your podcast is just as important as sharing episodes.

Collaboration is a powerful way to expand your reach. By partnering with other podcasters, you can tap into their audience while providing value to your own.

Reach out to podcasters in your niche and offer to be a guest on their show. Share your expertise or perspective on a topic that complements their content. Make sure to promote their podcast to your audience in return—it's a win-win.

Similarly, hosting guests on your podcast can attract new listeners. Choose guests who align with your audience's interests and have their own engaged following. When your episode goes live, encourage them to share it with their network.

Consider running a cross-promotion with another podcast. For example, you could trade short ad spots, with you promoting their show on your podcast and vice versa. This is especially effective when both podcasts have overlapping audiences.

Participate in online communities like Facebook groups, Reddit threads, or forums for podcasters. These spaces are great for networking, sharing tips, and finding collaboration opportunities.

Search Engine Optimization (SEO) isn't just for blogs and websites—it's a critical tool for helping new listeners discover your podcast. By optimizing your show notes, episode titles, and descriptions, you increase the chances of your podcast appearing in search results.

Your episode titles should be clear, descriptive, and include keywords that your target audience might search for. For example, instead of a vague title like "Episode 12: Productivity Tips," go for something like "5 Proven Strategies to Boost Your Productivity Today."

Show notes are an often-overlooked opportunity to improve SEO. Include a summary of your episode's content, relevant keywords, and timestamps for key topics. For example:

In this episode of *The Hustle Hour*, we discuss how to set effective goals, overcome procrastination, and achieve more in less time. Learn about the best tools for tracking your progress and hear success stories from our listeners.

Link to resources, articles, or tools mentioned in your episode. If you have a website or blog, include links to your other content. Backlinks from show notes help with SEO and provide additional value for your audience.

Most podcast directories display episode descriptions, so make them count. Write short, engaging summaries that highlight the value listeners will get from tuning in. Use keywords naturally and include a call to action, like subscribing or leaving a review.

Email remains one of the most direct and effective ways to connect with your audience. Unlike social media, where algorithms dictate visibility, emails land directly in your subscribers' inboxes.

Start a simple email newsletter where you share updates, announce new episodes, and provide exclusive content. Tools like Mailchimp or Substack make it easy to manage email campaigns, even for beginners.

Give listeners a reason to join your email list. For example:

- Share bonus content, like exclusive interviews or behind-the-scenes updates.
- Provide a free resource, such as a PDF guide, checklist, or ebook related to your podcast topic.

Email isn't just about promotion—it's about building relationships. Share personal stories, ask for feedback, and invite subscribers to reply to your emails. This two-way communication fosters loyalty and keeps your audience engaged.

Marketing isn't a one-time effort. It's an ongoing process of experimenting, analyzing results, and refining your approach.

Most podcast hosting platforms provide analytics that show download numbers, listener demographics, and episode performance. Use these insights to identify what's working and what needs adjustment. For example, if a certain topic resonates with your audience, consider creating more episodes on similar themes.

Not every tactic will work for every podcast, and that's okay. Test different approaches, like running paid ads, hosting live events, or creating short-form content for platforms like TikTok.

Above all, remember that growth takes time. Keep showing up, even if progress feels slow. The cumulative effect of your efforts will pay off in the long run.

Growing your podcast audience is a mix of strategy, persistence, and creativity. By using social media effectively, collaborating with other podcasters, and optimizing your content for discoverability, you'll steadily attract more listeners and build a loyal following. Remember, marketing isn't just about promoting your podcast—it's about creating genuine connections with the people who tune in. Keep experimenting, keep learning, and, most importantly, keep sharing your voice.

As podcasters, it's easy to fall into the trap of focusing solely on numbers. After all, metrics like downloads, followers, and rankings provide tangible ways to measure progress. But numbers, while important, only tell part of the story. The true success of your podcast lies not just in how many people listen but in how deeply you connect with them. Success is about engagement—how your audience interacts with your content—and growth, the steady evolution of your podcast over time.

When you first start podcasting, it's natural to watch your download numbers closely. They offer an immediate sense of feedback: Are people finding your episodes? Are your promotional efforts working? While these metrics can provide valuable insights, they don't capture the full picture. A podcast with a small but engaged audience can be far more impactful—and even profitable—than one with a large but passive listener base.

Instead of obsessing over hitting a specific number, focus on the relationships you're building. Are listeners leaving comments or reviews? Are they sharing your episodes with their friends? Are they reaching out with questions or feedback? These are signs that your podcast is resonating on a deeper level. Engagement is a far better indicator of long-term success than sheer volume.

Podcasting is not a sprint; it's a marathon. Growth often starts slow, and that's okay. The most successful podcasts rarely skyrocket overnight. They build their audience episode by episode, listener by listener, through consistent effort and a commitment to quality.

Consider the podcast *How I Built This* with Guy Raz. It's one of the most recognized shows today, but it didn't start with millions of downloads. The team focused on creating thoughtful, compelling content, and over time, their dedication paid off. Each episode added a layer to their reputation, drawing in more listeners and deepening their impact.

Your journey will likely follow a similar trajectory. Celebrate incremental growth—a few more downloads this month than last, a handful of new reviews, or an uptick in social media engagement. These small victories compound over time and pave the way for bigger milestones.

Engagement reflects the connection you have with your audience, and that connection is what keeps listeners coming back. Here's how to measure and cultivate engagement:

- **Listener Feedback:** Pay attention to comments, messages, and emails from your audience. If people are taking the time to reach out, it means your content is making an impression.

- **Social Shares:** When listeners share your episodes on social media, they're not just engaging—they're endorsing your podcast to their network. This kind of organic promotion is invaluable.

- **Reviews and Ratings:** Positive reviews are a sign that your content resonates with your audience. Even critical feedback can be an opportunity to learn and improve.

- **Interaction in Communities:** If your podcast inspires conversations in online forums, social media groups, or your own listener community, you're fostering engagement that goes beyond the episodes themselves.

Focus on these moments of connection. They're proof that your podcast is making an impact, and they're far more meaningful than download numbers alone.

Success looks different for every podcaster. For some, it's about building a loyal audience of thousands. For others, it's about reaching a niche group of listeners who deeply value the content. Maybe your goal is to educate, entertain, or inspire. Maybe it's to promote your business or explore a passion. Whatever your vision, let it guide how you measure success.

For example, if you host a wellness podcast, your success might be reflected in messages from listeners who've implemented your advice and seen positive changes in their lives. If you're a true-crime podcaster, success might mean creating an episode that sparks meaningful discussions about justice. Define your goals clearly, and remind yourself of them often. They'll keep you grounded when numbers feel overwhelming.

Growth doesn't need to be exponential to be impactful. One of the most rewarding aspects of podcasting is the cumulative effect of your efforts. Each episode builds on the last, each listener has the potential to share your content, and each improvement you make enhances the experience for your audience.

The compound effect is real. Even small, steady growth adds up over time. If you gain just ten new listeners a month, by the end of the year, you'll have added 120 people to your audience. And if those listeners are engaged—sharing your content, leaving reviews, or supporting your podcast financially—that growth has a ripple effect.

Podcasting is more than a numbers game. It's about sharing your voice, telling your story, and making a difference in the lives of your listeners. It's about the email you receive from a listener who says your podcast inspired them, the review that thanks you for shedding light on a difficult topic, or the comment that says, "I feel like you're speaking directly to me."

These moments of connection are immeasurable, but they're the real indicators of success. They remind you why you started podcasting in the first place and motivate you to keep going, even when growth feels slow.

As you navigate the ups and downs of building your audience, remember to stay focused on what matters most: creating valuable, meaningful content. Your listeners are tuning in because they believe in what you're offering. Honor that trust by continuing to show up and deliver your best work.

Yes, metrics can be useful—they help you refine your strategy and understand what's working. But they're just one piece of the puzzle. Don't let numbers overshadow the bigger picture of what you're creating and why it matters.

Every podcaster starts somewhere. Whether you have 10 listeners or 10,000, you're on a journey of growth, creativity, and connection. Celebrate the progress you've made, the audience you've built, and the impact you've had so far. Each step forward is a success in itself.

As you move forward, let engagement and growth be your guiding lights. They're the true markers of a podcast that's making a difference. Numbers will rise and fall, but the relationships you build with your listeners are what will sustain your podcast for the long haul.

Your voice matters, your content matters, and your journey matters. Keep showing up, keep sharing, and trust that the growth will come. After all, the best things in podcasting—like in life—are worth the wait.

Getting Started in Podcasting

Chapter 10: Sustaining Your Podcast Journey

Starting a podcast is exhilarating. You launch your first episodes with a mix of nerves and excitement, fueled by creative energy and big dreams. But as time goes on, the reality of podcasting settles in—it's not just about hitting "record." Consistency, audience growth, and maintaining enthusiasm can feel like a full-time commitment. This is where many podcasters face challenges like podfade or burnout. The initial thrill gives way to the weight of responsibility, and the question looms: *How do I keep going?*

First, let's normalize these struggles. Almost every podcaster has faced moments of doubt or exhaustion. *Podfade*, the term for podcasts that slowly lose momentum and stop releasing episodes, is common. In fact, studies show that the majority of podcasts don't make it past 10 episodes. But the good news is, many podcasters also find ways to reignite their passion and push through. By learning to navigate these pitfalls, you can sustain your podcast and continue creating something meaningful.

Podfade typically happens gradually. You miss a week here, then two weeks. Before long, the idea of recording another episode feels overwhelming, and the podcast quietly slips into inactivity. The causes can vary—lack of time, diminishing enthusiasm, or even feelings of imposter syndrome.

Burnout, on the other hand, is more intense. It happens when the pressures of podcasting feel insurmountable. Maybe you're juggling too many responsibilities, striving for perfection in every episode, or feeling disappointed by slow growth. Burnout doesn't just threaten your podcast—it can impact your mental health and creativity.

These challenges are real, but they're also surmountable. Many successful podcasters have been where you are, questioning whether to keep going. What separates those who persevere from those who fade out is a willingness to adapt, reassess, and find joy in the process again.

Consider the journey of *The Minimalists Podcast*, hosted by Joshua Fields Millburn and Ryan Nicodemus. In their early days, they juggled podcasting with other commitments, often struggling to find time for consistent episodes. Instead of giving up, they simplified their process, allowing their podcast to grow alongside their other projects. Today, it's a cornerstone of their brand, reaching millions of listeners.

Or take *Lore* by Aaron Mahnke. Despite its immense popularity now, Aaron faced periods of doubt early on, unsure if his niche storytelling would resonate. He leaned into his passion for crafting eerie narratives, focusing on what he loved rather than chasing trends. That authenticity carried him through moments of uncertainty, and *Lore* is now a global phenomenon with books, TV adaptations, and live shows.

These stories highlight an important truth: challenges don't mean failure. They're opportunities to recalibrate, rediscover your purpose, and keep moving forward. The key is to recognize the warning signs early and take proactive steps to sustain your podcasting journey.

Every podcaster faces obstacles, but those obstacles don't have to define your journey. By embracing the ups and downs, you're not just sustaining a podcast—you're building something resilient and impactful.

Podcasting is often described as a marathon, not a sprint. The excitement of launching your show and gaining initial listeners can sustain you for the first few months, but what happens when the novelty wears off? Staying motivated for the long haul requires a combination of strategy, creativity, and adaptability. Let's explore some actionable tips to help you keep your podcasting journey rewarding and fulfilling.

One of the most effective ways to avoid burnout and maintain momentum is by planning and scheduling episodes in advance. When you have a clear roadmap, podcasting becomes less overwhelming and more structured.

Recording multiple episodes in one session can be a game-changer. It reduces the pressure of weekly recording and gives you a buffer for busy weeks. For example, you might set aside one weekend a month to record three or four episodes. This way, even if life gets hectic, your podcast schedule stays consistent.

An editorial calendar is your secret weapon for long-term podcast planning. Use it to map out topics, guest appearances, and publishing dates for the next few months. By organizing your ideas in advance, you can maintain a steady flow of content and avoid the stress of last-minute brainstorming.

Leverage automation tools to handle repetitive tasks. For instance, many podcast hosting platforms allow you to schedule episodes in advance, so you don't need to manually publish them. Similarly, social media scheduling tools like Buffer or Hootsuite can handle promotions for upcoming episodes, freeing up your time to focus on content creation.

Your audience isn't just a group of passive listeners—they're your community. Actively engaging with them can reignite your passion for podcasting and remind you why you started in the first place.

Encourage your audience to share their thoughts, ask questions, or suggest topics for future episodes. This not only strengthens your connection with listeners but also provides a treasure trove of ideas for new content. For example, you might dedicate a segment of your show to answering listener questions or discussing their feedback.

Consider hosting live Q&A sessions on social media platforms like Instagram or YouTube. These events allow you to connect with your audience in real-time, fostering a sense of community and excitement around your podcast. Additionally, you can create polls or surveys to gauge what your listeners want to hear next.

Acknowledge your audience's role in your podcast's success. Whether it's reading a heartfelt review during an episode or giving shoutouts to loyal listeners, these gestures show that you value their support. Some podcasters even dedicate entire episodes to listener stories or experiences, creating a deeply engaging and participatory format.

Even the most passionate podcaster can feel stuck in a rut if the content starts to feel repetitive. To keep your creativity flowing, focus on evolving your format and exploring new ideas.

If your show primarily features interviews, try incorporating solo episodes, roundtable discussions, or listener call-ins. Mixing up the format not only keeps things interesting for your audience but also challenges you to grow as a creator.

Inviting guest experts, co-hosts, or even members of your audience to contribute to episodes can bring new energy to your podcast. Their unique insights and experiences can spark conversations that take your show in exciting directions.

Listening to other podcasts, reading books, or attending industry events can inspire new ideas for your content. Pay attention to what resonates with you as a listener or reader and consider how you can incorporate similar elements into your podcast.

Sometimes, a simple refresh can make a big difference. Update your podcast artwork, add a new segment to your episodes, or experiment with different intro music. These changes signal to your audience—and to yourself—that your podcast is constantly evolving.

Podcasting isn't just about delivering content; it's also about growing as a creator. By setting personal goals and embracing a growth mindset, you can maintain your enthusiasm and stay motivated.

Break your podcasting journey into smaller, manageable goals. For example, aim to reach 1,000 downloads, secure your first guest, or experiment with a new editing technique. Celebrating these milestones keeps you motivated and reinforces your progress.

Take time to sharpen your skills, whether it's improving your interviewing techniques, mastering audio editing software, or learning more about storytelling. Many podcasters find renewed excitement when they challenge themselves to grow and improve.

Revisit the reasons you started your podcast. Was it to share your passion, connect with like-minded people, or build your personal brand? Keeping your "why" front and center can help you stay focused and motivated, even when challenges arise.

Finally, remember that it's okay to take breaks or adjust your approach. Podcasting is a creative endeavor, and creativity requires space and balance.

No episode will ever be perfect, and that's okay. Your audience is more interested in your authenticity than in polished production. Give yourself permission to embrace imperfections and focus on the value you're providing.

If you're feeling overwhelmed, it's better to take a planned break than to push through burnout. Communicate with your audience about the hiatus and let them know when to expect new episodes. They'll appreciate your honesty and come back when you're ready.

Sometimes, sustaining motivation is as simple as acknowledging how far you've come. Whether you've released five episodes or fifty, you've accomplished something worth celebrating. Reflect on the connections you've made, the skills you've developed, and the impact you've had on your listeners.

Sustaining motivation as a podcaster isn't about avoiding challenges—it's about embracing them as part of the journey. By planning ahead, engaging with your audience, and evolving your content, you can keep your passion for podcasting alive and thriving. Each episode you create is a testament to your dedication and creativity, and your audience is lucky to have you as their guide. Remember, podcasting isn't just a project; it's a journey, and the most rewarding moments often come when you least expect them.

Podcasting is more than a medium; it's a journey. When you embark on this path, you're not just creating episodes—you're building something that can resonate deeply with others, something that has the potential to make a real impact. While the challenges of consistency, creativity, and growth can sometimes feel overwhelming, the rewards of podcasting far outweigh the difficulties. Every episode you produce, every listener you reach, and every story you share contributes to something larger than yourself: a legacy of connection and influence.

Think about your favorite podcasts and the role they've played in your life. Maybe they've inspired you to try something new, given you a sense of comfort during tough times, or introduced you to ideas that changed your perspective. Now, consider this: your podcast has the potential to do the same for someone else.

Each time you hit record, you're creating a ripple effect. Your voice reaches listeners who might share your content with friends, apply your insights to their lives, or even start a podcast of their own. These ripples extend further than you can see, touching lives in ways you might never fully understand. It's this power—the ability to connect with people on a personal level—that makes podcasting so rewarding.

Take, for example, *The Happiness Lab* with Dr. Laurie Sartos. What started as an exploration of the science of well-being has grown into a global phenomenon, helping countless listeners reframe their understanding of happiness. Or *Armchair Expert* with Dax Shepard, a show that brings vulnerability and humor to conversations about life's complexities. These podcasters didn't start with the goal of massive reach; they started with the intention to share something meaningful—and the audience followed.

Podcasting is unique in that it allows you to share your voice and vision with the world in an unfiltered, authentic way. Unlike other forms of content creation, there's no need for elaborate production or a massive budget. All you need is your voice, your message, and the willingness to show up.

This accessibility democratizes creativity. You don't need to be a celebrity or have a background in media to start a podcast. You just need to care deeply about what you're sharing. Whether your podcast helps listeners navigate personal challenges, learn new skills, or simply enjoy a moment of laughter, you're creating something that matters.

Remember, your podcast doesn't need to appeal to everyone to be successful. The most impactful shows often cater to niche audiences. By focusing on what you're passionate about and speaking directly to the people who care, you create a loyal community of listeners who value your work. It's not about reaching millions—it's about reaching the right people.

Podcasting isn't just about what you give to others—it's also about what you gain. Every episode you create is an opportunity to grow as a communicator, storyteller, and creator. You'll learn to articulate your thoughts more clearly, explore new ideas, and connect with people you might never have met otherwise.

This personal growth is one of podcasting's greatest rewards. It's not just about building an audience; it's about building yourself. Over time, you'll look back on your early episodes and see how far you've come—not just in technical skill, but in confidence, creativity, and vision.

And as you grow, so does your impact. Your listeners aren't just numbers on a dashboard—they're real people whose lives you're touching. Maybe it's the parent who listens to your parenting tips while driving their kids to school, the entrepreneur who applies your advice to grow their business, or the student who feels less alone because of your stories.

These connections are the heart of podcasting, and they're what make all the effort worthwhile.

It's easy to get caught up in goals like reaching a certain number of downloads, landing a sponsorship deal, or climbing the charts on Apple Podcasts. While these milestones can be exciting, they're not the ultimate measure of success. The true reward of podcasting lies in the process itself—the act of creating, sharing, and connecting.

Think of your podcasting journey as an adventure. There will be high points, like receiving heartfelt messages from listeners, and low points, like technical mishaps or slow audience growth. But every step, every episode, and every lesson learned is part of a bigger picture. It's the sum of these experiences that makes podcasting so meaningful.

As you navigate this journey, don't forget to celebrate your progress. Every episode you publish is an achievement. Every listener you gain is someone who chose to spend their time with you. These moments, big and small, are worth acknowledging and cherishing.

One of the most beautiful things about podcasting is its permanence. Once an episode is published, it exists as a resource that people can discover and revisit for years to come. Your voice, your insights, and your stories have the potential to outlive the moment of their creation, continuing to inspire and influence long after you've moved on to new projects.

This lasting impact is a reminder that podcasting isn't just about the present—it's about contributing to something enduring. The episodes you create today could be the catalyst for someone else's journey tomorrow. By sharing your voice, you're leaving a legacy that matters.

Podcasting is a rewarding journey, but it's not without its challenges. There will be days when motivation wanes, when growth feels slow, or when you question whether it's all worth it. In those moments, remind yourself why you started. Think about the listeners who look forward to your episodes, the lives you're impacting, and the joy you feel when you create something meaningful.

Keep showing up. Keep sharing your voice. The rewards of podcasting aren't always immediate, but they're real and lasting. Whether your audience is a dozen loyal listeners or a global community, your work matters. You're making a difference, one episode at a time.

Podcasting is a journey of creativity, connection, and growth. It challenges you to think deeply, communicate clearly, and share authentically. Along the way, you'll touch lives, build relationships, and create something uniquely yours. So as you move forward, embrace the adventure. Celebrate the progress. And trust that the impact of your podcast will ripple out in ways you can't yet imagine.

Your voice matters. Your story matters. And your podcasting journey is just beginning.

A Word from the Author

First and foremost, thank you for picking up this book. Whether you're just starting out or looking to take your podcast to the next level, I'm honored that you've chosen to spend your time with my words. Podcasting is a unique and exciting adventure, and I'm thrilled to play even a small part in your journey.

This book is the result of countless hours of research, observation, and trial and error—not just my own, but from learning alongside podcasters who've shared their triumphs and struggles. My hope is that the strategies, tips, and insights within these pages empower you to navigate the podcasting world with confidence and creativity.

Remember, every successful podcaster started somewhere. Every loyal audience, impactful episode, or incredible milestone began with a single recording and a simple idea: to share something meaningful with the world. No matter where you are on your journey, you have something valuable to offer. Your unique voice, perspective, and passion are what will make your podcast stand out.

Podcasting is as much about the experience as it is about the outcomes. It's about connecting with people, sharing your story, and enjoying the process of growth. There will be challenges, but there will also be moments of incredible joy and fulfillment. Stay dedicated, embrace the lessons, and never stop learning.

I wish you the best of luck as you hit that "Record" button and start building something truly special. Whether your goal is to share your passion, create a thriving community, or even make podcasting a career, you've got what it takes to succeed.

Here's to your podcasting journey—may it be full of discovery, creativity, and connection.

Jordan Vance